Cooking
for Special
Occasions

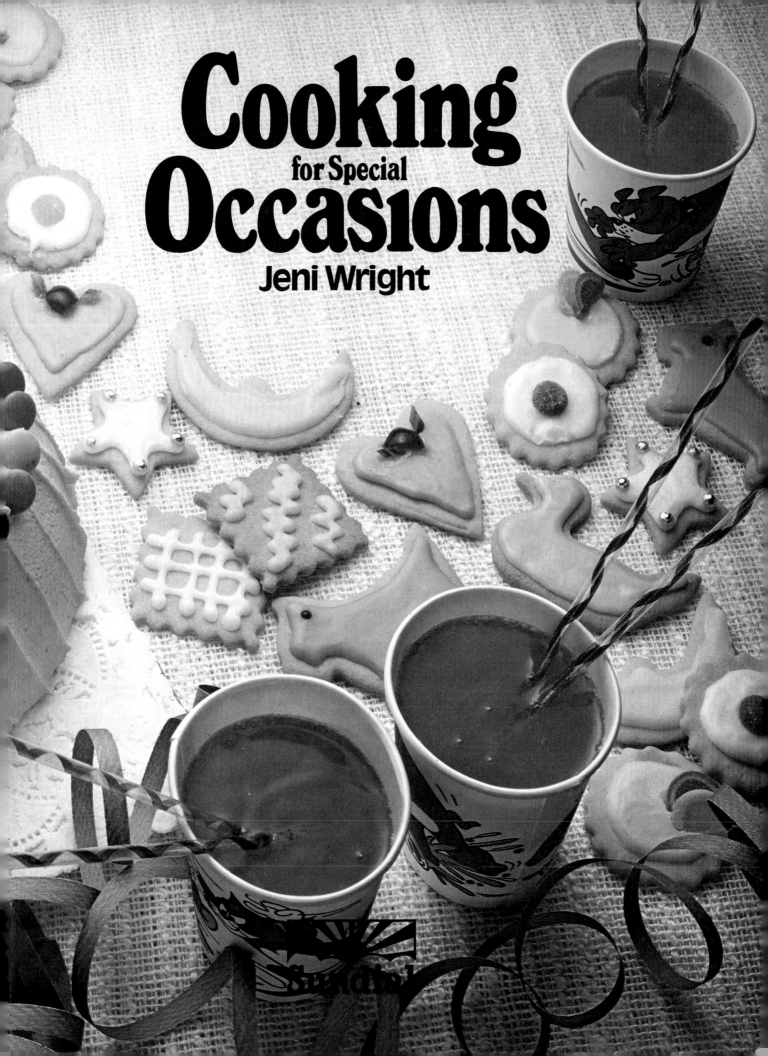

Cooking
for Special
Occasions
Jeni Wright

Sundial

Contents

First published in 1977 by Sundial Books Limited
59 Grosvenor Street, London W1

© 1977 Hennerwood Publications Limited

ISBN 0 904230 49 X

Printed in England by Severn Valley Press Limited

Gone are the days when a wine and cheese party meant cubes of pineapple and cheese on sticks and a few bottles of plonk! A party with a theme such as this gives the host or hostess plenty of scope to be imaginative, particularly with the immense variety of English and imported cheeses that are available.

In addition to the dishes you choose to cook for the party, you will also want to offer your guests a good cheeseboard. When choosing cheeses for this make sure that your selection includes both hard and soft, and blue cheeses, as well as a number of the more unusual and attractive kinds such as the French cheeses that are covered in grape seeds or halved walnuts. Goat's cheese comes in a variety of shapes and sizes—and is also quite different in flavour from cheese made with cow's milk—therefore these would add interest.

Arrange different colours and textures together to make an eye-catching board, and serve with a selection of unusual biscuits, crackers and crispbreads, as well as French and granary breads. Bowls of crisp, fresh fruit add colour and also complement the texture of cheese. Most of the recipes serve between ten and fifteen people as part of a buffet party spread.

Spinach and cheese quiche

Metric

For the pastry:
100 g plain white flour
Pinch of salt
100 g wholemeal flour
100 g butter or margarine
About 4 × 15 ml spoons cold water to mix

For the filling:
350 g cottage cheese, sieved
1 whole egg, beaten
3 egg yolks, beaten
150 ml soured cream
½ teaspoon grated nutmeg
Salt and freshly ground black pepper
3 × 226 g packets frozen chopped spinach, thawed
50 g Cheddar cheese, grated
½ teaspoon cayenne pepper

Imperial

For the pastry:
4 oz plain white flour
Pinch of salt
4 oz wholemeal flour
4 oz butter or margarine
About 4 tablespoons cold water to mix

For the filling:
12 oz cottage cheese, sieved
1 whole egg, beaten
3 egg yolks, beaten
¼ pint soured cream
½ teaspoon grated nutmeg
Salt and freshly ground black pepper
3 × 8 oz packets frozen chopped spinach, thawed
2 oz Cheddar cheese, grated
½ teaspoon cayenne pepper

Cooking Time: 50 minutes
Oven: 200°C, 400°F, Gas Mark 6

To make the pastry: Sieve the plain flour and salt into a mixing bowl. Stir in the wholemeal flour. Add the butter or margarine in pieces and rub into the flour until the mixture resembles fine breadcrumbs. Stir in enough cold water to draw the mixture together. Form into a ball, wrap in foil or greaseproof paper and chill in the refrigerator for at least 30 minutes before using.

Roll out the dough on a floured board and use to line a 28 cm (11 in) flan tin or flan ring, placed on a baking sheet. Prick the base with a fork. Line the dough with foil, fill with baking beans and bake blind in a fairly hot oven for 10 minutes, then remove beans and foil and continue baking for a further 5 minutes. Remove from oven and set aside.

To prepare filling: put the cottage cheese, eggs and soured cream in a bowl and mix well to combine. Stir in half the nutmeg and salt and pepper to taste. Put the spinach in the base of the pastry case, sprinkle with salt and pepper and the remaining nutmeg, then pour over the cottage cheese mixture. Mix the grated Cheddar cheese with the cayenne pepper and sprinkle over the quiche.

Bake in a fairly hot oven for approximately 35 minutes until the filling is set and the cheese topping is golden. Remove from the oven and serve warm, cut into wedges. Cuts into 16 wedges

Swiss cheese fondue; Spinach and cheese quiche

Swiss cheese fondue

Metric

1 garlic clove, peeled
and cut in half
600 ml dry white wine
2 × 5 ml spoons lemon
juice
450 g Emmenthal cheese,
grated
450 g Cheddar cheese,
grated
2 × 15 ml spoons
cornflour
1 miniature bottle (4 ×
15 ml spoons) Kirsch
Pinch of cayenne pepper
Freshly ground black
pepper
1–2 long French loaves
cut into 2·5 cm cubes

Imperial

1 garlic clove, peeled
and cut in half
1 pint dry white wine
2 teaspoons lemon
juice
1 lb Emmenthal cheese,
grated
1 lb Cheddar cheese,
grated
2 tablespoons
cornflour
1 miniature bottle (4
tablespoons) Kirsch
Pinch of cayenne pepper
Freshly ground black
pepper
1–2 long French loaves
cut into 1 in cubes

Remember to tell your guests the old Swiss saying that if one of the gentlemen guests drops his cube of bread in the fondue pot, then he must buy the next bottle of wine; if a lady drops her cube of bread, then she must kiss all the men present. Traditionally, Swiss fondue is made with both Emmenthal and Gruyère cheeses; this recipe substitutes Cheddar for the Gruyère, and is therefore less expensive.

Rub the garlic around the inside of a heavy-based saucepan, then discard. Add the wine and lemon juice and heat gently, then gradually stir in the Emmenthal and Cheddar cheeses, a little at a time. Stir constantly until both cheeses are melted and thoroughly combined with the wine. Mix the cornflour to a paste with the Kirsch, then stir slowly into the cheese mixture. Heat gently until the fondue bubbles and thickens, stirring constantly. Add the cayenne, and black pepper to taste. Pour the fondue into a heated fondue pot and keep hot over a low flame, stirring occasionally. Serve with cubes of French bread. (Guests should spear cubes of bread on fondue forks and dip these into the fondue pot until thoroughly coated in the cheese).
Serves 8–10

Devilled crab dip

Metric	Imperial
350 g cream cheese	12 oz cream cheese
4–6 × 15 ml spoons thick homemade mayonnaise (see page 20)	4–6 tablespoons thick homemade mayonnaise (see page 20)
2 × 5 ml spoons chilli sauce	2 teaspoons chilli sauce
2 × 5 ml spoons Worcestershire sauce	2 teaspoons Worcestershire sauce
Salt and freshly ground black pepper	Salt and freshly ground black pepper
1 medium-sized cucumber, peeled, seeded and finely diced	1 medium-sized cucumber, peeled, seeded and finely diced
Pinch of sugar	Pinch of sugar
150 g packet frozen crabmeat, thawed	5 oz packet frozen crabmeat, thawed
¼ teaspoon cayenne pepper	¼ teaspoon cayenne pepper

This is a light creamy dip with a peppery bite. For a stronger flavour of crab, the quantity of crabmeat given here may be doubled.

Beat the cream cheese with a wooden spoon until soft, then gradually beat in the mayonnaise until a soft, creamy consistency is obtained. Stir in the sauces, and salt and pepper to taste.

Sprinkle the diced cucumber with the sugar and stir into the cheese mixture, then fold in the crabmeat. Taste and adjust seasoning, then spoon into a serving bowl, sprinkle with the cayenne pepper and chill in the refrigerator before serving.

Serves about 10

Blue cheese dip

Metric	Imperial
50 g unsalted butter, softened	2 oz unsalted butter, softened
350 g Gorgonzola cheese, rind removed and softened	12 oz Gorgonzola cheese, rind removed and softened
About 6 × 15 ml spoons milk	About 6 tablespoons milk
4 sticks of celery, trimmed, scrubbed and finely chopped	4 sticks of celery, trimmed, scrubbed and finely chopped
75 g walnuts, finely chopped	3 oz walnuts, finely chopped
Freshly ground black pepper	Freshly ground black pepper

The Gorgonzola cheese in this dip gives it a strong flavour, and a little will go a long way.

Whip the butter with an electric or rotary beater until light and soft, then gradually beat in the cheese a little at a time until thoroughly combined. Gradually stir in the milk until a creamy consistency is obtained, then fold in three-quarters of the celery and one-third of the walnuts. Add black pepper to taste and transfer to a serving bowl. Combine the remaining celery and walnuts and sprinkle over the top of the dip. Chill in the refrigerator before serving.

Serves about 12

Serve chilled dips in shallow bowls with a selection of crisp raw vegetables, savoury biscuits and crisps for 'dipping'. Guests can then help themselves.

Blue cheese dip; Devilled crab dip; Hot cheese and herb loaf

Hot cheese and herb loaf

Metric

1 long French loaf
50 g butter
225 g cream cheese,
softened
2 × 15 ml spoons finely
chopped parsley
2 × 15 ml spoons
snipped chives
2 × 15 ml spoons finely
chopped thyme, marjoram
or basil
Salt and freshly ground
black pepper

Imperial

1 long French loaf
2 oz butter
8 oz cream cheese,
softened
2 tablespoons finely
chopped parsley
2 tablespoons snipped
chives
2 tablespoons finely
chopped thyme, marjoram
or basil
Salt and freshly ground
black pepper

Cooking Time: 15 minutes
Oven: 200°C, 400°F, Gas Mark 6

Cut the loaf in half lengthwise and spread the inside cut surfaces with butter. Beat the cream cheese with the herbs until thoroughly combined, adding salt and pepper to taste.

Spread the cheese mixture on the butter, dividing it equally between each half. Put the loaf back together again, wrap in foil, then place directly on oven shelf. Bake in a fairly hot oven for 10 minutes, open the foil wrapping and continue baking for a further 5 minutes or until the loaf is crisp and the cheese is hot.

Remove from the oven, discard foil, cut loaf into thick slices and transfer to a bread basket or board.

Serve immediately

To freeze: freeze in foil wrapping before baking, over-wrap in a freezer bag.

To thaw: bake in foil wrapping from frozen in a fairly hot oven for 10 minutes, then open foil wrapping and bake until crisp and heated through.

Cuts into 12–14 slices

Celery and walnut salad

Metric

*2 large heads of celery,
trimmed, scrubbed and
roughly chopped
50 g walnuts, chopped
4 satsumas or mandarin
oranges, peeled,
divided into segments
and pith removed
6 crisp dessert apples
1 × 15 ml spoon lemon
juice
300 ml natural yogurt
1 × 5 ml spoon caraway
seeds
Salt and freshly ground
black pepper*

Imperial

*2 large heads of celery,
trimmed, scrubbed and
roughly chopped
2 oz walnuts, chopped
4 satsumas or mandarin
oranges, peeled,
divided into segments
and pith removed
6 crisp dessert apples
1 tablespoon lemon
juice
½ pint natural yogurt
1 teaspoon caraway
seeds
Salt and freshly ground
black pepper*

Put the celery, walnuts and satsumas or mandarins in a mixing bowl and stir to combine. Peel and core the apples, then chop roughly. Sprinkle immediately with the lemon juice to prevent discoloration and stir into the celery and walnut mixture. Stir in the yogurt, caraway seeds, and salt and pepper to taste, then mix well to combine. Taste and adjust seasoning, transfer to a serving bowl and chill in the refrigerator until serving time.
Serves 12–15

Winter salad

Metric

*1 firm white cabbage
(about 1 kg), shredded
3 large carrots, peeled
and grated
50 g sultanas
100 g dates, pitted and
roughly chopped
225 g Edam or Gouda
cheese, rind removed
and diced*

For the dressing:
*6 × 15 ml spoons corn or
vegetable oil
2 × 15 ml spoons lemon
juice
2 × 15 ml spoons clear
honey
Salt and freshly ground
black pepper*

Imperial

*1 firm white cabbage
(about 2 lb), shredded
3 large carrots, peeled
and grated
2 oz sultanas
4 oz dates, pitted and
roughly chopped
8 oz Edam or Gouda
cheese, rind removed
and diced*

For the dressing:
*6 tablespoons corn or
vegetable oil
2 tablespoons lemon
juice
2 tablespoons clear
honey
Salt and freshly ground
black pepper*

Put the cabbage, carrots, sultanas, dates and cheese in a mixing bowl and stir well to combine. Put the ingredients for the dressing in a screw-topped jar and shake well. Pour the dressing over the salad and toss until thoroughly coated. Taste and adjust seasoning, transfer to a serving bowl and toss again before serving.
Serves about 12

Celery and walnut salad; Winter salad; Salata Inglese

Salata inglese

Metric

For the dressing:
6 × 15 ml spoons olive oil
2 × 15 ml spoons red wine
vinegar
1 × 15 ml spoon Meaux
mustard
Salt and freshly ground
black pepper

For the salad:
2 curly endives, washed
and broken into sprigs
2 large green peppers,
cored, seeded and finely
sliced
2 heads of fennel, trimmed
and finely sliced
2 hard-boiled eggs, finely
sieved
175 g Stilton cheese,
rind removed

Imperial

For the dressing:
6 tablespoons olive oil
2 tablespoons red wine
vinegar
1 tablespoon Meaux
mustard
Salt and freshly ground
black pepper

For the salad:
2 curly endives, washed
and broken into sprigs
2 large green peppers,
cored, seeded and finely
sliced
2 heads of fennel, trimmed
and finely sliced
2 hard-boiled eggs, finely
sieved
6 oz Stilton cheese,
rind removed

Put the dressing ingredients, with salt and pepper to taste, in a large salad bowl and beat well with a fork until thick. Add the salad vegetables and eggs to the bowl, crumble over the cheese, then mix gently together until salad and cheese are lightly coated in the dressing. Taste and adjust seasoning and serve immediately.
Serves 10–12

Punch; Glühwein

Punch

Metric	Imperial
1 litre bottle rosé wine	1 litre bottle rosé wine
8 × 15 ml spoons rum	8 tablespoons rum
2 × 15 ml spoons sugar, or to taste	2 tablespoons sugar, or to taste
1 large orange, sliced, pips discarded	1 large orange, sliced, pips discarded
1 lemon, sliced, pips discarded	1 lemon, sliced, pips discarded
1 cinnamon stick, broken in two	1 cinnamon stick, broken in two
Pinch of grated nutmeg	Pinch of grated nutmeg
4 cloves	4 cloves

Cooking Time: 10–15 minutes

A good drink for Christmas or New Year celebrations. Serve hot in stoneware goblets or heatproof tumblers. Pour the wine and rum into a large saucepan, add the sugar and heat gently until the sugar dissolves. Float remaining ingredients on top of punch and heat gently for 10 to 15 minutes. Do not allow to boil. Taste for sweetness, then strain and serve hot with orange and lemon slices in glasses or goblets.

Fills about 8 glasses

Glühwein

Metric	Imperial
1 litre bottle dry red wine	1 litre bottle dry red wine
300 ml water	½ pint water
2 × 15 ml spoons sugar, or to taste	2 tablespoons sugar, or to taste
1 cinnamon stick, broken in two	1 cinnamon stick, broken in two
1 bay leaf	1 bay leaf
1 lemon stuck with a few cloves	1 lemon stuck with a few cloves

Cooking Time: 10–15 minutes

A simple Austrian version of mulled wine, Glühwein is the ideal drink to serve with cheese.

Pour the wine and water into a large saucepan, add the sugar and heat gently until the sugar dissolves. Float the remaining ingredients on top of Glühwein and heat gently for 5 to 10 minutes. Do not allow to boil. Taste for sweetness, then strain and serve hot in heatproof glasses or stoneware goblets.

Fills 8–10 glasses

Fresh fruit brûlée

Fresh fruit brûlée

Metric

For the sugar syrup:
100 g sugar
300 ml water
2 × 15 ml spoons
Cointreau or brandy

For the fruit salad:
4 crisp eating apples
2 large bananas
225 g black grapes,
halved and depipped
4 peaches, peeled, halved,
stoned and sliced
4 pears, peeled, cored and
sliced
50 g blanched almonds,
split and toasted

For the topping:
300 ml double or
whipping cream
25 g vanilla sugar
100–175 g soft brown
sugar

Imperial

For the sugar syrup:
4 oz sugar
½ pint water
2 tablespoons
Cointreau or brandy

For the fruit salad:
4 crisp eating apples
2 large bananas
8 oz black grapes,
halved and depipped
4 peaches, peeled, halved,
stoned and sliced
4 pears, peeled, cored and
sliced
2 oz blanched almonds,
split and toasted

For the topping:
½ pint double or
whipping cream
1 oz vanilla sugar
4–6 oz soft brown
sugar

Cooking Time: 15 minutes

The fresh fruit in this dessert will vary considerably from season to season, depending on the availability of fruit. Obviously the best season will be the summer, although good fruit salads can be made in the winter with the help of dried fruits and nuts.

To prepare sugar syrup: put the sugar and water in a saucepan and heat gently, without stirring, until the sugar has dissolved. Increase the heat and boil rapidly for approximately 5 minutes until the mixture is syrupy. Remove pan from the heat and leave sugar syrup to cool. Stir in the Cointreau or brandy.

Peel, core and slice the apples and put in a shallow heatproof serving dish. Peel the bananas and slice thinly, add to the apples with the grapes, peaches and pears. Pour over the sugar syrup, folding it into the fruit with the almonds. Be careful not to break or bruise the fruit. Whip the cream with the vanilla sugar until thick, then spoon over the fruit in the dish to cover it. Sprinkle the brown sugar evenly over the cream and put under a preheated hot grill for approximately 5 minutes until the sugar has caramelised. Remove from the grill, leave to cool, then refrigerate until serving time.

Serves 8–10

A small buffet party for around 20 people is the ideal
way to entertain relatives and friends informally, and
is particularly suitable for such occasions as
Christenings and Silver or Golden Wedding celebrations.
When planning the menu for your buffet party, try to
choose dishes that allow guests to help themselves. Try
also to provide food that can be eaten easily with the
fingers or a fork, as most of the guests will probably
be standing to eat, and may have to hold a glass of
wine or champagne at the same time.
The recipes in this chapter can all be eaten with a
fork, or a spoon in the case of desserts.

Finger and fork platter

Stuffed cucumbers, eggs and tomatoes, celery boats and
mushroom caps look both attractive and colourful when
arranged on platters for a buffet table, and guests can
easily help themselves. Try to keep individual items as
small as possible so that they can be eaten in one or two
mouthfuls, but provide plates and forks in case some of
the guests prefer not to eat with their fingers.

Stuffed tomatoes
Cut 8 firm but ripe tomatoes in half. Scoop out the flesh
carefully with a teaspoon (this can be used in soups or
casseroles, if liked.) Sieve 225 g (8 oz) cottage cheese and
mix with 100 g (4 oz) finely chopped boiled ham and 1 × 5
ml spoon (1 teaspoon) Tabasco sauce (or to taste).
Season well with salt and freshly ground black pepper.
Spoon the filling into the tomato cases, mounding it in
the centre. Cut 16 stoned olives in quarters and arrange
in a flower motif on top of the cottage cheese mixture.
Makes 16 halves

Mushroom caps
You will need 450 g (1 lb) deep cup-shaped mushrooms
for these. Wipe them clean and carefully break the stalks
from the caps. Fry the caps gently in a little butter for
1 minute on each side. Chop the stalks finely and fry
until golden in a little butter with 1 medium-sized onion,
peeled and finely chopped, and 50 g (2 oz) fine white
breadcrumbs. Transfer to a mixing bowl and stir in
100 g/4 oz finely chopped garlic sausage. Spoon into
the mushroom caps, sprinkle with 50 g (2 oz) grated
Parmesan cheese, and cayenne pepper to taste, and put
under a hot grill for a few minutes until golden brown.
Transfer to a serving platter, leave until cold, then
sprinkle liberally with finely chopped parsley.

Celery boats
Trim the stalks of 1 large head of celery, scrub thoroughly
and cut into 5 cm (2 in) lengths. Beat 225 g (8 oz) cream
cheese until soft with a wooden spoon, then stir in 2 ×
15 ml spoons (2 tablespoons) anchovy essence, 50 g (2 oz)
finely chopped walnuts, and freshly ground black pepper
to taste. Fill mixture into celery pieces and sprinkle with
a little paprika pepper.

Stuffed eggs
Halve 12 hard-boiled eggs lengthwise, scoop out the
yolks carefully and mash with a fork. Mix with 150 ml
($\frac{1}{4}$ pint) thick homemade mayonnaise (see page 20), 1 × 15
ml spoon (1 tablespoon) curry paste (or to taste), salt and
freshly ground black pepper to taste. Pipe into the
reserved egg whites and decorate each with a slice of
stuffed olive.
Makes 24 halves

Cucumber canoes
Trim 2 cucumbers and score the length of each with the
prongs of a fork. Cut in half lengthwise, scoop out the
flesh from the inside, place in a sieve, sprinkle with salt
and leave to drain for 30 minutes. Pat dry with absorbent
kitchen paper, then mix with 175 g (6 oz) roughly chopped
peeled prawns, 3 × 15 ml spoons (3 tablespoons) thick
mayonnaise and 2 × 15 ml spoons (2 tablespoons) snipped
chives. Season liberally with salt and freshly ground
black pepper. Cut each cucumber half into approximately
6 'canoes', spoon in the filling and sprinkle each one with
a little cayenne pepper.
Makes 24

Danish pork and prune open sandwiches

Metric

5 large slices of white bread, crusts removed
Butter for spreading
198 g can Danish cured pork
113 g carton cottage cheese with chives
Salt and freshly ground black pepper
10 prunes, halved and pitted
10 large orange slices, peel, pith and pips removed

Imperial

5 large slices of white bread, crusts removed
Butter for spreading
7 oz can Danish cured pork
4 oz carton cottage cheese with chives
Salt and freshly ground black pepper
10 prunes, halved and pitted
10 large orange slices, peel, pith and pips removed

The three recipes on these two pages are all variations of Danish open sandwiches and should be made as small as possible for easy eating. Arrange different toppings on the same platter for an eye-catching, mouth-watering spread. Use day old bread or the toppings will not adhere to their bases, and pierce each 'sandwich' with a cocktail stick, if you like. Garnish the platter with sprigs of watercress or parsley if liked.

Spread the bread with plenty of butter and cut each slice neatly into quarters with a sharp knife. Cut the pork lengthwise into 10 slices, then cut each slice in half. Place one slice of pork on each piece of bread, and cut to the same size if necessary. Put 1 heaped 5 ml spoon (1 heaped teaspoon) cottage cheese on each quarter and sprinkle with salt and pepper. Place a prune half on top of the cottage cheese and press down firmly, then cut the orange slices into quarters and arrange two quarters on either side of the prunes to form a 'butterfly'.
Makes 20

Mackerel salad open sandwiches

Metric

6 large slices of rye or wholemeal bread
Butter for spreading
2 × 120 g cans mackerel fillets in tomato sauce, flaked
2 × 5 ml spoons lemon juice
2 × 15 ml spoons mayonnaise
Freshly ground black pepper

To garnish:
4 hard-boiled eggs, sliced
24 gherkins, drained

Imperial

6 large slices of rye or wholemeal bread
Butter for spreading
2 × 4¼ oz cans mackerel fillets in tomato sauce, flaked
2 teaspoons lemon juice
2 tablespoons mayonnaise
Freshly ground black pepper

To garnish:
4 hard-boiled eggs, sliced
24 gherkins, drained

Spread the bread with plenty of butter, then cut neatly into quarters with a sharp knife. Mix the flaked mackerel with the lemon juice, mayonnaise and pepper to taste, then spread on the buttered bread, dividing the mixture equally among the quarters. Decorate the top of each quarter with a slice of egg and a gherkin fan.

To make gherkin fans: slice gherkin into four lengthwise, keeping gherkin in one piece at the base. Spread the four slices out in a fan shape, holding the base firmly.
Makes 24

Danish open sandwiches:
Garlic sausage and cheese; Mackerel salad; Danish pork and prune

Garlic sausage and cheese open sandwiches

Metric

*227 g packet (7 slices)
pumpernickel bread
100 g cream cheese
Salt and freshly ground
black pepper
28 thin slices of garlic
sausage, rind removed
28 pimiento-stuffed green
olives, cut in halves*

Imperial

*8 oz packet (7 slices)
pumpernickel bread
4 oz cream cheese
Salt and freshly ground
black pepper
28 thin slices of garlic
sausage, rind removed
28 pimiento-stuffed green
olives, cut in halves*

Cut the pumpernickel slices into quarters and spread each one thickly with the cream cheese. Sprinkle with salt and pepper to taste. Fold each slice of garlic sausage in half, then cut almost in two. Twist each half in opposite directions then place on the cream cheese, pressing down gently to adhere. Arrange an olive half on each side of the sausage. Sprinkle with more salt and pepper.
Makes 28

Avocado mousse

Metric	Imperial
1 × 15 ml spoon powdered gelatine	1 tablespoon powdered gelatine
150 ml chicken stock	¼ pint chicken stock
2 ripe avocados	2 ripe avocados
2 × 15 ml spoons lemon juice	2 tablespoons lemon juice
150 ml thick homemade mayonnaise (see page 20)	¼ pint thick homemade mayonnaise (see page 20)
150 ml double cream	¼ pint double cream
1 × 5 ml spoon Worcestershire sauce	1 teaspoon Worcestershire sauce
Dash of Tabasco sauce	Dash of Tabasco sauce
Salt and freshly ground pepper	Salt and freshly ground pepper

To garnish:
1 green pepper, cored, seeded and finely chopped
1 red pepper, cored, seeded and finely chopped
Few 15 ml spoons well-flavoured vinaigrette dressing

To garnish:
1 green pepper, cored, seeded and finely chopped
1 red pepper, cored, seeded and finely chopped
Few tablespoons well-flavoured vinaigrette dressing

Light in texture, yet rich to eat, this mousse makes a couple of avocados go a long way. Do not unmould until just before ready to serve or the avocados will discolour. Sprinkle the gelatine over the stock in a small heatproof bowl and leave to stand until spongy. Put the bowl in a pan of hot water and stir over low heat until the gelatine has dissolved. Remove from the heat and leave to cool. Peel and halve the avocados and discard the stones. Mash the flesh with a fork and stir in the lemon juice immediately to prevent discoloration. Stir in the cooled gelatine stock until well mixed, then fold in the mayonnaise.

Whip the cream until thick, then fold into avocado mixture, mixing in the Worcestershire and Tabasco sauces at the same time. Season to taste.

Pour the mixture into a lightly oiled 900 ml (1½ pint) ring mould and chill in the refrigerator for several hours or overnight until set. Unmould on to a serving plate: hold an inverted plate over the top of the mousse, then turn the mould over.

Fill the centre of the mousse with the red and green peppers tossed in the vinaigrette dressing.

To freeze: freeze mousse in the ring. Wrap in foil, then overwrap in a freezer bag. Seal, label and freeze.

To thaw: leave in wrappings in the refrigerator overnight, then turn out, fill the centre of mousse and serve immediately.

Serves 8–10

Smoked salmon quiche

Metric	Imperial
For the pastry:	For the pastry:
225 g flour	8 oz flour
Pinch of salt	Pinch of salt
125 g butter	4 oz butter
3–4 × 15 ml spoons cold water to mix	3–4 tablespoons cold water to mix
For the filling:	For the filling:
225 g cream cheese, softened	8 oz cream cheese, softened
4 egg yolks, beaten	4 egg yolks, beaten
4 whole eggs, beaten	4 whole eggs, beaten
175 g smoked salmon, slivered	6 oz smoked salmon, slivered
2 × 15 ml spoons lemon juice	2 tablespoons lemon juice
About 300 ml milk or single cream	About ½ pint milk or single cream
½ teaspoon cayenne pepper	½ teaspoon cayenne pepper
Freshly ground black pepper	Freshly ground black pepper

Cooking Time: 35 minutes
Oven: 190°C, 375°F, Gas Mark 5

To make the pastry: sieve flour and salt into a bowl, add butter in pieces and rub into flour until mixture resembles fine breadcrumbs. Stir in enough cold water to draw mixture together, form into a ball, wrap in foil and chill in the refrigerator for at least 30 minutes. Roll out the dough on a floured board and use to line a 28 cm (11 in) flan tin. Chill for a further 15 minutes.

Meanwhile, make the filling: put the cream cheese in a large mixing bowl and gradually beat in the eggs a little at a time. Stir in the smoked salmon, then add the lemon juice, and enough milk or cream to give the mixture a soft consistency. Stir in the cayenne, and black pepper to taste. Pour the filling into the chilled flan case, place on a preheated baking sheet and bake in a fairly hot oven for 35 minutes until the filling is set and the pastry golden. Remove from the oven and leave until cold before cutting into wedges to serve.

To freeze: wrap cold quiche in cling film or foil, then overwrap in a freezer bag. Seal, label and freeze.

To thaw: leave in wrappings in the refrigerator overnight.

Cuts into 16 wedges

Avocado mousse; Smoked salmon quiche; Pâté au citron

Pâté au citron

Metric

350 g piece boned, skinned ham shank
6 juniper berries
6 black peppercorns
1 bay leaf
225 g pig's liver, minced
350 g pie (stewing) veal, minced
1 small onion, peeled and finely chopped
1 garlic clove, peeled and crushed
50 g fresh white breadcrumbs
4 × 15 ml spoons lemon juice
1 × 5 ml spoon freshly chopped tarragon; or ½ teaspoon dried tarragon
1 egg, beaten
Salt and freshly ground black pepper
3 lemons, cut into thin slices, pips removed

To garnish:
Watercress sprigs

Imperial

12 oz piece boned, skinned ham shank
6 juniper berries
6 black peppercorns
1 bay leaf
8 oz pig's liver, minced
12 oz pie (stewing) veal, minced
1 small onion, peeled and finely chopped
1 garlic clove, peeled and crushed
2 oz fresh white breadcrumbs
4 tablespoons lemon juice
1 teaspoon freshly chopped tarragon; or ½ teaspoon dried tarragon
1 egg, beaten
Salt and freshly ground black pepper
3 lemons, cut into thin slices, pips removed

To garnish:
Watercress sprigs

Cooking Time: 2 hours
Oven: 160°C, 325°F, Gas Mark 3

Put the ham, juniper berries, peppercorns and bay leaf in a saucepan and cover with water. Bring to the boil, then lower the heat, half cover with a lid and simmer gently for approximately 1 hour or until the ham is tender. Remove from the heat and leave to cool. Remove the ham from the cooking liquid and mince finely into a mixing bowl. Add the remaining ingredients, except the lemon slices, and stir well until thoroughly combined. Lightly oil the base and sides of a 1 kg (2 lb) loaf tin or earthenware pâté or casserole dish and line with the lemon slices, arranging them as close together as possible. Spoon the pâté mixture into the tin or dish, packing it down well and smoothing with a wooden spoon. Cover with foil and stand in a bain marie (water bath) of hot water. Bake in a warm oven for approximately 2 hours until the pâté is firm and has shrunk away from the sides of the tin or dish. Remove from the bain marie, put heavy weights on top of pâté and leave until completely cold. Turn pâté out on to a serving board or platter and garnish with sprigs of watercress. One or two slices of pâté may be cut before serving, if liked.

Herb and garlic breads

Metric	Imperial
1 long French loaf	1 long French loaf
100 g butter, softened	4 oz butter, softened
4 × 15 ml spoons finely chopped herbs (parsley, chives, marjoram)	4 tablespoons finely chopped herbs (parsley, chives, marjoram)

Cooking Time: 15 minutes
Oven: 200°C, 400°F, Gas Mark 6

Cut the bread into 2·5 cm (1 in) thick slices without cutting right through the base. Cream the butter and herbs together in a bowl until thoroughly combined, then spread on the cut surfaces of the bread.

Wrap the loaf in foil, place directly on oven shelf and bake in a fairly hot oven for 10 minutes, then open the foil wrapping and continue baking for a further 5 minutes or until the loaf is crisp. Remove from the oven, unwrap and serve hot.

To freeze: prepare as above, wrap in foil, seal label and freeze.

To thaw: reheat from frozen in foil wrapping, allowing 5–10 minutes extra cooking time.

Variation

Garlic bread
Prepare as for herb bread, substituting 2 garlic cloves, peeled and crushed, for the herbs.

Beetroot salad

Metric	Imperial
1 kg cooked beetroot, skinned and diced	2 lb cooked beetroot, skinned and diced
100 g walnuts, finely chopped	4 oz walnuts, finely chopped
4 × 15 ml spoons creamed horseradish sauce	4 tablespoons creamed horseradish sauce
4 × 15 ml spoons fresh orange juice	4 tablespoons fresh orange juice
Salt and freshly ground black pepper	Salt and freshly ground black pepper
150 ml soured cream	¼ pint soured cream
2 × 15 ml spoons snipped chives	2 tablespoons snipped chives

This colourful salad is simple to make. It has a sharp 'bite' which contrasts well with the richness of the Chicken Mayonnaise or Smoked Salmon Quiche.

Put the beetroot and walnuts in a large mixing bowl and stir in the horseradish sauce and orange juice. Mix thoroughly and season to taste with salt and pepper. Transfer the salad to a serving bowl. Beat the soured cream with a fork until evenly mixed, then trickle over the beetroot. Sprinkle with chives and chill in the refrigerator until serving time.
Serves 15

Mayonnaise

Metric	Imperial
1 egg yolk	1 egg yolk
Pinch of dry English mustard	Pinch of dry English mustard
Salt and freshly ground black pepper	Salt and freshly ground black pepper
150 ml vegetable or olive oil	¼ pint vegetable or olive oil
2 × 15 ml spoons lemon juice	2 tablespoons lemon juice

When making mayonnaise it is essential to have all the ingredients and utensils at room temperature, or the egg and oil may separate. If separation does occur, start again with a fresh egg yolk, gradually stir in the separated mixture once the mayonnaise is made, then add more oil and lemon juice.

Put the egg yolk, mustard, and salt and pepper to taste in a mixing bowl. Add the oil a drop at a time, beating well after each addition with a fork, electric or rotary beater. When the mayonnaise begins to thicken, add the oil more quickly and eventually pour it into the bowl in a thin steady stream.

When all the oil is incorporated, beat in the lemon juice. Taste and adjust seasoning. Cover and store in the refrigerator until required. Let it stand at room temperature before use.

Herb and garlic breads; Beetroot salad; Mayonnaise

Chicken mayonnaise

Metric	Imperial
1 × 2 kg roasting chicken	1 × 4 lb roasting chicken
1 garlic clove, peeled and cut in half	1 garlic clove, peeled and cut in half
50 g butter, melted	2 oz butter, melted
1 × 5 ml spoon dried tarragon	1 teaspoon dried tarragon
Salt and freshly ground black pepper	Salt and freshly ground black pepper
150 ml dry white wine	¼ pint dry white wine
150 ml thick homemade mayonnaise (see page 20)	¼ pint thick homemade mayonnaise (see page 20)
150 ml double cream	¼ pint double cream
3 × 15 ml spoons sweet mango chutney	3 tablespoons sweet mango chutney
2 red dessert apples	2 red dessert apples
1 green dessert apple	1 green dessert apple
1 × 15 ml spoon lemon juice	1 tablespoon lemon juice
100 g blanched almonds, roughly chopped	4 oz blanched almonds, roughly chopped
4 large oranges, peeled and sliced into rings, pith and pips removed	4 large oranges, peeled and sliced into rings, pith and pips removed

Cooking Time: 1½ hours
Oven: 190°C, 375°F, Gas Mark 5

This salad of chicken pieces in a sauce of mayonnaise and cream looks very attractive when served on a bed of pilaf. See below.

Remove the skin from the chicken, rub the flesh with the garlic, then place garlic inside the bird. Brush the bird with butter, sprinkle with tarragon and season liberally. Put the chicken on its side in a roasting tin, pour in the wine and roast in a fairly hot oven for approximately 1½ hours or until the chicken is tender, turning it over on to its other side and its back during the cooking time and basting occasionally. When the chicken is cooked, remove from the oven and leave to cool, then carve into small neat slices or strips.

Put the chicken in a large mixing bowl and fold in the mayonnaise, half the cream and the chutney. Core the apples, slice thinly into bite-sliced pieces and sprinkle with the lemon juice to prevent discoloration. Mix into the chicken and mayonnaise mixture with half the almonds. Fold gently until all the chicken and apple pieces are coated lightly in the mayonnaise, then taste and adjust seasoning. Arrange the pilaf (see recipe below) on a large serving platter, place the orange slices in a single layer in the centre of the rice and spoon the chicken mayonnaise on to the oranges, leaving a border of oranges around the chicken. Trickle the remaining cream in a line down the centre of the chicken and scatter the remaining almonds on top.
Serves 10

Pilaf

Metric	Imperial
50 g butter	2 oz butter
1 large onion, peeled and finely chopped	1 large onion, peeled and finely chopped
2 large sticks celery, trimmed, scrubbed and finely chopped	2 large sticks celery, trimmed, scrubbed and finely chopped
450 g long-grain rice	1 lb long-grain rice
About 750 ml hot chicken stock	About 1¼ pints hot chicken stock
Salt and freshly ground black pepper	Salt and freshly ground black pepper
1 large green pepper, cored, seeded and finely chopped	1 large green pepper, cored, seeded and finely chopped
50 g seedless raisins	2 oz seedless raisins

Cooking Time: 30–35 minutes
Oven: 190°C, 375°F, Gas Mark 5

Cooking rice in larger quantities than given here can be tricky, therefore if more is required it is best to make several casseroles of this size, rather than attempting to cook all the rice in one dish.

Melt the butter in a flameproof casserole dish. Add the onion and celery and cook gently until soft and lightly coloured. Add the rice to the pan and fry until it begins to turn colour, stirring occasionally with a wooden spoon. Pour in 600 ml (1 pint) of the hot stock all at once, bring to the boil, add salt and pepper to taste, stir once, then cover with buttered greaseproof paper and a lid and transfer to a fairly hot oven.

Cook for 30 minutes or until the rice is tender and all the stock has been absorbed. Check the level of the stock after 20 minutes of cooking time, adding more hot stock if the rice is becoming dry. Remove from the oven, leave until cold, then gently fold in the green pepper and raisins. Taste and adjust seasoning. Arrange on a large serving platter and serve with Chicken Mayonnaise (see above).
Serves 10

Chicken mayonnaise with pilaf; Italian salad

Italian salad

Metric

1½ *kg firm, ripe tomatoes,
skinned and quartered*
½ *teaspoon sugar*
*225 g garlic sausage,
rinds removed and
thickly sliced*
*100 g black olives,
halved and pitted*
*225 g mozarella cheese,
diced*
*4 × 15 ml spoons olive
oil*
*2 × 15 ml spoons lemon
juice*
*1 × 5 ml spoon French
mustard*
*Salt and freshly ground
black pepper*
*1 large onion, peeled and
thinly sliced*
*2 × 15 ml spoons finely
chopped basil or parsley*

Imperial

*3 lb firm, ripe tomatoes,
skinned and quartered*
½ *teaspoon sugar*
*8 oz garlic sausage,
rinds removed and
thickly sliced*
*4 oz black olives,
halved and pitted*
*8 oz mozarella cheese,
diced*
*4 tablespoons olive
oil*
*2 tablespoons lemon
juice*
*1 teaspoon French
mustard*
*Salt and freshly ground
black pepper*
*1 large onion, peeled and
thinly sliced*
*2 tablespoons finely
chopped basil or parsley*

The large continental varieties of tomatoes are ideal for this salad, and are normally available during the summer months. If Italian mozarella is not obtainable, the Danish equivalent can be substituted.

Put the quartered tomatoes in a large serving bowl and sprinkle with sugar. Cut each slice of garlic sausage into small pieces, add to the bowl with the olives and cheese and stir gently to mix. In a separate bowl whisk together the oil and lemon juice until thick, then whisk in the mustard and salt and pepper to taste. Pour this dressing over the tomato salad, add the onion and basil or parsley and mix gently until the salad is thoroughly coated in dressing and herbs. Taste and adjust seasoning, then cover and chill in the refrigerator until serving time.

Note: If preparing salad ahead of time, do not add dressing, onion and herbs until just before serving.
Serves 12

23

Cheesecake with grapes

Metric

200 g packet plain
chocolate digestive
biscuits
50 g roasted hazelnuts,
finely chopped
75 g butter, melted

For the filling:
350 g black or green
grapes, halved and depipped
700 g cream cheese
2 eggs, beaten
100 g caster sugar
2 × 15 ml spoons honey
Finely grated rind and
juice of 1 lemon

Imperial

7 oz packet plain
chocolate digestive
biscuits
2 oz roasted hazelnuts,
finely chopped
3 oz butter, melted

For the filling:
12 oz black or green
grapes, halved and depipped
1½ lb cream cheese
2 eggs, beaten
4 oz caster sugar
2 tablespoons honey
Finely grated rind and
juice of 1 lemon

Cooking Time: 1¼ hours
Oven: 150°C, 300°F, Gas Mark 2

The addition of lemon and the garnish of grapes make this rich dessert tangy and refreshing.

Put the biscuits between two sheets of greaseproof paper and crush finely with a rolling pin. Put in a mixing bowl with the hazelnuts and melted butter and stir to combine. Using a metal spoon, press into the base and sides of a lightly oiled 18 cm (7 in) loose-bottomed springform pan. Chill in the refrigerator for at least 1 hour until set. Put a layer of grapes, cut side down, in the bottom of the pan, arranging them as close together as possible. Reserve the remaining grapes for decorating the top of the finished cheesecake.

Beat the cream cheese in a bowl until light and fluffy, then beat in the eggs a little at a time. Fold in the sugar, reserving 2 × 15 ml spoons (2 tablespoons), then the honey, lemon rind and juice.

Pour this mixture over the grapes in the pan, then place on a baking sheet and bake in a cool oven for approximately 1¼ hours or until the filling is set. Turn off the oven, leave cheesecake in the oven until completely cold, then transfer to the refrigerator and chill overnight.

Remove cheesecake carefully from pan and transfer to a serving platter. Arrange the reserved grapes in a circular pattern on the top and sprinkle with the remaining sugar.

To freeze: cool cheesecake after cooking, remove springform part of pan, leaving cheesecake standing on base. Open freeze until firm, then carefully ease the cheesecake off the base. Wrap loosely in foil, then overwrap in a large freezer bag. Seal, label and freeze.

To thaw: unwrap, place on a serving dish and leave in the refrigerator overnight.

Decorate with grapes after thawing.

Serves 10–12

Cheesecake with grapes

Strawberries romanoff

Metric

700 g–1 kg strawberries,
hulled and washed
100 g caster sugar, or
to taste
6 × 15 ml spoons vodka
3 × 15 ml spoons black
cherry jam
1½ × 15 ml spoons
powdered gelatine
3 × 15 ml spoons water
600 ml double or
whipping cream

Imperial

1½–2 lb strawberries,
hulled and washed
4 oz caster sugar, or
to taste
6 tablespoons vodka
3 tablespoons black
cherry jam
1½ tablespoons
powdered gelatine
3 tablespoons water
1 pint double or
whipping cream

This is a light, creamy mixture of strawberries and cream. The addition of gelatine holds the mixture together without setting it as it would in a traditional soufflé. Purée 225 g (8 oz) strawberries and 50 g (2 oz) sugar in an electric blender until smooth. Transfer to a mixing bowl. Mix the vodka and cherry jam until evenly blended, then stir into the strawberry purée.

Slice the remaining strawberries, reserving a few whole ones for decoration, put in a shallow bowl and sprinkle with more caster sugar (the amount needed will depend on the sweetness of the strawberries). Set aside.

Sprinkle the gelatine over the water in a small heatproof bowl and leave to stand until spongy. Put the bowl in a pan of hot water and stir over low heat until the gelatine has dissolved. Remove from the heat, leave to cool slightly then stir into the strawberry purée. Leave to stand until the purée begins to thicken. Whip the cream until thick, reserving a few spoonfuls for decoration, then fold into the purée until evenly distributed. Gently stir in the sliced strawberries, pour into a glass serving bowl and chill in the refrigerator until serving time. Decorate with the whole strawberries and piped rosettes of whipped cream just before serving.

To freeze: freeze without decoration in the serving bowl if it will withstand the low freezer temperature, or transfer to a rigid container. Cover, label and freeze.

To thaw: leave in wrappings in the refrigerator overnight. Decorate after thawing and serve chilled.

Serves 10–12

Strawberries romanoff

Anniversary cake

Metric	Imperial
350 g butter or margarine	12 oz butter or margarine
350 g soft brown sugar	12 oz soft brown sugar
6 eggs, beaten	6 eggs, beaten
350 g flour	12 oz flour
Pinch of salt	Pinch of salt
1 × 5 ml spoon baking powder	1 teaspoon baking powder
1 × 5 ml spoon mixed spice	1 teaspoon mixed spice
1 × 5 ml spoon grated nutmeg	1 teaspoon grated nutmeg
1 × 5 ml spoon ground cinnamon	1 teaspoon ground cinnamon
350 g sultanas	12 oz sultanas
350 g currants	12 oz currants
225 g seedless raisins	8 oz seedless raisins
100 g mixed candied peel	4 oz mixed candied peel
175 g glacé cherries, finely chopped	6 oz glacé cherries, finely chopped
75 g blanched almonds, finely chopped	3 oz blanched almonds, finely chopped
Finely grated rind and juice of 1 lemon	Finely grated rind and juice of 1 lemon
4 × 15 ml spoons brandy, rum or sherry	4 tablespoons brandy, rum or sherry
700 g Almond Paste (see page 44)	1½ lb Almond Paste (see page 44)

Cooking Time: 3½ hours
Oven: 170°C, 325°F, Gas Mark 3

Grease a 23 cm (9 in) square cake tin and line with a double layer of greaseproof paper. Brush with oil.

Beat the butter until soft and light, add the sugar and cream together until light and fluffy. Beat in the eggs a little at a time, adding a little of the measured flour if the mixture shows signs of separating. Sieve the flour with the salt, baking powder and spices into a large mixing bowl. Stir in the dried fruit, candied peel, glacé cherries and almonds and mix thoroughly. Fold into the butter and sugar, adding the lemon rind and juice and half the spirits. Mix well together, then spoon into the prepared tin. Spread level.

Bake in a warm oven for 3½ hours or until a skewer inserted in the centre of the cake comes out clean. Cover the cake with foil if it becomes too brown during cooking. When cooked, remove from the oven and leave to cool slightly. Prick a few holes in the top of the cake with a skewer and spoon over the remaining spirits. Leave until cold, then turn out of the tin and remove the greaseproof paper. Wrap in aluminium foil and store in an airtight tin for at least a month to improve the flavour, spooning over more spirits from time to time, if wished. Cover with Almond Paste before icing and decorating.

Royal icing

Metric	Imperial
3 egg whites	3 egg whites
450–700 g icing sugar, sieved	1–1½ lb icing sugar, sieved
1 × 15 ml spoon glycerine	1 tablespoon glycerine
Yellow or blue food colouring	Yellow or blue food colouring

The icing is applied to this cake by 'flooding'—this method makes it easier to obtain a smooth surface than by the more conventional 'flat' icing. Always keep icing covered while not in use or it will become hard and impossible to use.

Put the egg whites in a clean bowl and break up with a fork. Add the icing sugar a little at a time, beating well with a wooden spoon after each addition. Keep adding the icing sugar until the icing is smooth and coats the back of the spoon, then stir in the glycerine. Stir gently for a few minutes to reduce air bubbles.

Pour the icing into an airtight container and cover with a lid, or cover the bowl with a damp cloth and place in a polythene bag. Leave to stand for several hours, preferably overnight. Next day, stir the icing gently to reduce air bubbles.

Put 4 × 15 ml spoons (4 tablespoons) icing in a separate bowl, cover with a lid or damp cloth and set aside in a cool place. Colour the remaining icing blue for a silver wedding cake, yellow for a golden wedding cake. Stand the cake on a wire rack over a tray and pour all the icing on to the top of the cake. Gently lift and tip the tray to make the icing flow evenly down the sides of the cake and use a palette knife to help make the icing cover the entire surface of the cake. Gently prick any air bubbles that form on the surface of the icing, working quickly before the icing begins to dry. Immediately scoop up the surplus icing, put in a bowl and cover with a lid or damp cloth. Leave both cake and icing in a cool place overnight.

The next day, run a sharp pointed knife around the base of the cake to make sure that it is free of the wire rack. Put a few blobs of icing on a 28 cm (11 in) square silver cake board, pick up the cake using the flat of your hands on the sides and place it on the board.

Anniversary cake

Sugar roses

Metric

1½ × 5 ml spoons
powdered gelatine
30 ml boiling water
About 500 g icing
sugar, sieved
Few drops of food
colouring (optional)

Imperial

1½ teaspoons powdered
gelatine
2 fl oz boiling water
About 1 lb 2 oz icing
sugar, sieved
Few drops of food
colouring (optional)

Dissolve the gelatine in the boiling water. Stir in enough icing sugar to make a firm putty-like paste and add food colouring if wished. If storing, keep in polythene.

Pinch out small pieces of paste to form petals, dipping your fingers in a little cornflour as you work. Wrap these petals around a pyramid of paste, using a little water to make them stick. Make a large rose with eight or ten large petals for the centre of the design, then make smaller roses with fewer petals, grading them down to rosebuds with only three or four petals. Cut off the bases of the pyramids at an angle and press on to the cake with small blobs of icing.

To decorate the cake

1. Make a plain greaseproof paper cone and cut it at the end. Thicken the reserved white icing with the remaining icing sugar and put a little in the cone. Mark an 18 cm (7 in) circle on top of the cake with this icing, then pipe a plain line over the marks to draw in the circle.

2. Draw the outline of the figures '25' or '50', in the centre of the circle, using the same paper cone and more of the icing. If wished, you can use bought numerals.

3. Cut the end of the cone to make a leaf point, put in a little more icing and pipe a garland of leaves on top of the circular line. (Bought silver or gold leaves may be fixed between these piped leaves for added effect.)

4. Using the same leaf-pointed cone, pipe a double row of leaves around the base of the cake, one row on the cake, the other on the board. Pipe a few leaves up the sides.

5. Thin down the remaining icing with a little water to a running consistency, put in a small paper cone and use to fill in the numerals in the centre of the circle.

If you are planning to cater for a wedding buffet, it is likely to be the most important event for which you ever have to cook, and you will want to be sure that such a special occasion is going to be a success. It is essential to plan your menu several weeks before the day of the buffet. When you have decided on the number of guests to be invited—and they have accepted the invitations—you will have to work out the quantities needed. Each recipe in this chapter has the number of servings at the bottom of the method, therefore you can easily gauge how many dishes you will need to make for the number of guests that are coming.

Canapes

Ideally, canapés should be small enough to eat in one or two bites. Remove crusts from white, wholemeal or granary bread, toast lightly on both sides and cut slices into halves or quarters or stamp into small rounds with a pastry cutter after toasting. As an alternative to toasting, the bread can be lightly fried in butter—but be sure to drain well on absorbent kitchen paper before using. If preferred, the canapé base can be made of savoury cheese pastry—use any recipe for cheese straws, or see recipe for Cheesy Sausage Rolls on page 88. Roll the pastry out thinly and stamp into 6 cm (2½ in) or 7·5 cm (3 in) rounds and other shapes with a pastry cutter. Another alternative is to use crispbreads, crackers and savoury biscuits as bases. For an eye-catching spread, combine different shapes, textures and toppings on large serving platters and top with a selection of the following:

Cream cheese toppings
Mix 100 g (4 oz) softened cream cheese with:
1. 50 g (2 oz) pimiento-stuffed green olives, finely chopped. Season to taste. Spread on to buttered canapés and top with 1 slice of stuffed olive.
2. 25 g (1 oz) finely chopped walnuts and ½ teaspoon cayenne pepper. Season to taste. Spread on to buttered canapés and top each with half a walnut.
3. Half a cucumber, peeled, seeded and finely chopped. Season to taste. Spread on to buttered canapés and top each with a generous sprinkling of snipped chives.
4. 50 g/2 oz pitted dates, finely chopped. Season to taste. Spread on to buttered canapés.
5. Four rashers of crisply fried streaky bacon, rinds removed, finely chopped. Season to taste. Spread on to buttered canapés and top with two strips of green pepper.

Salmon topping
Drain a 225 g (8 oz) can red salmon and flake with a fork. Fold lightly into 4 × 15 ml spoons/4 tablespoons mayonnaise blended with a few drops of Tabasco sauce. Spread on to buttered canapés, sprinkle with a little cayenne pepper and garnish with watercress sprigs.

Sardine topping
Drain a 124 g (4½ oz) can sardines in olive oil. Mash well with a fork and combine with 2 × 5 ml spoons (2 teaspoons) lemon juice and 2 × 15 ml spoons (2 tablespoons) mayonnaise or natural yogurt. Season the mixture with plenty of freshly ground black pepper. Refrigerate for 30 minutes or until needed, then spread on to butter-fried canapés and top each with 2 small onion rings and 1 small parsley sprig.

Tuna topping
Drain a 198 g (7 oz) can tuna and flake with a fork. Fold lightly into 4 × 15 ml spoons (4 tablespoons) soured cream and season well with salt and freshly ground black pepper. Spread on to buttered canapés and top each with a gherkin fan (see recipe for Mackerel Salad, page 16).

Savoury butters
Combine 100 g (4 oz) softened butter with any one of the following, blending well with a wooden spoon. Spread or pipe on to canapés and refrigerate until serving time.
Anchovy: Drain a 50 g (2 oz) can anchovies in olive oil, cover with milk and leave to soak for 30 minutes. Drain well, pound to a paste with a pestle and mortar and blend into butter, with freshly ground black pepper to taste.
Blue cheese: Soften 50 g (2 oz) Danish Blue/Gorgonzola cheese with a wooden spoon. Blend into butter.
Watercress: Chop 1 bunch watercress very finely and blend into butter. Season with plenty of salt. This butter is an attractive bright green in colour.
Chilli: Blend 3 × 15 ml spoons (3 tablespoons) chilli relish and the finely grated rind of ½ lemon into the butter, with salt and pepper to taste.

Chicken and mushroom vol-au-vents

Metric	Imperial
2 × 405 g packets frozen puff pastry, thawed	2 × 14·3 oz packets frozen puff pastry, thawed
2 eggs, beaten	2 eggs, beaten
For the filling:	For the filling:
40 g butter	1½ oz butter
225 g button mushrooms, cleaned and finely chopped	8 oz button mushrooms, cleaned and finely chopped
40 g flour	1½ oz flour
450 ml hot milk	¾ pint hot milk
150 ml double cream	¼ pint double cream
½ teaspoon ground mace	½ teaspoon ground mace
Salt and freshly ground black pepper	Salt and freshly ground black pepper
350 g cooked chicken meat, finely diced	12 oz cooked chicken meat, finely diced
To garnish:	To garnish:
Parsley sprigs	Parsley sprigs

Cooking Time: 15 minutes
Oven: 200°C, 400°F, Gas Mark 6

Roll out the dough thinly on a floured board and stamp into 40 rounds with a 7·5 cm (3 in) fluted pastry cutter. Place the rounds on dampened baking sheets and brush with beaten egg. Stamp circles on the rounds with a 5 cm (2 in) cutter, without cutting right through the dough. Bake in a fairly hot oven for approximately 15 minutes or until well risen and golden.

Meanwhile, make the filling: melt the butter in a pan, add the mushrooms and cook gently for 2 minutes until the juices flow. Stir in the flour and cook for a further 1 to 2 minutes, stirring constantly. Remove the pan from the heat and gradually add the hot milk, stirring vigorously with a wooden spoon. Return the pan to the heat and bring slowly to the boil, stirring constantly. Lower the heat and simmer gently until the sauce thickens. Remove from the heat and leave to cool for 1 to 2 minutes, then stir in the double cream, mace and salt and pepper to taste. Fold in the chicken meat, return the pan to a very low heat and cook gently until hot.

Taste and adjust for seasoning. Remove the pastry cases from the oven, leave to cool slightly, then remove the tops with a sharp knife and reserve. Scoop out any soft pastry with a teaspoon, spoon the filling into each vol-au-vent and replace reserved tops. Garnish each vol-au-vent with a small sprig of parsley, transfer to a warmed serving platter and serve immediately.

To freeze: freeze pastry cases separately from filling. Open freeze unbaked cases until firm, then pack in rigid containers, separating layers with foil. Seal, label and return to freezer. Pour cooled filling into rigid containers. Seal, label and freeze.

To thaw: unwrap pastry cases, place on baking sheets and brush with beaten egg. Stand at room temperature for 30 minutes, then bake in a hot oven (220°C, 425°F, Gas Mark 7) for 20 minutes. Reheat filling in a saucepan, stirring occasionally. Fill pastry cases with hot filling as for fresh vol-au-vents above.
Makes 40

Salted nuts

Metric	Imperial
6 × 15 ml spoons corn oil	6 tablespoons corn oil
75 g butter	3 oz butter
450 g shelled mixed nuts (almonds, peanuts, cashews, walnuts, etc.)	1 lb shelled mixed nuts (almonds, peanuts, cashews, walnuts, etc.)
Salt	Salt

Cooking Time: 5 minutes

These make a nutritious nibble with drinks before the buffet food is served.

Heat the oil and butter in a skillet or frying pan until foaming. Add the nuts and fry for 5 minutes, shaking the pan, until browned on all sides. Remove from pan with a slotted spoon and drain well on absorbent kitchen paper. Sprinkle with salt to taste, allow to cool, then heap into serving dishes or bowls.

Devilled Nuts are a hot spicy version prepared as above with the addition of 1 × 5 ml spoon (1 teaspoon) cayenne pepper with the salt.

Other nibbles may be made with dates, prunes and walnuts, stuffed or sandwiched together with well-seasoned softened cream cheese.

Vol-au-vents; Smoked salmon rolls; Stuffed dates; Salted nuts

Smoked salmon rolls

Metric	Imperial
For the horseradish cream:	For the horseradish cream:
150 ml double cream	¼ pint double cream
2 × 15 ml spoons grated horseradish or horseradish sauce	2 tablespoons grated horseradish or horseradish sauce
1 × 5 ml spoon wine vinegar	1 teaspoon wine vinegar
Salt and freshly ground black pepper	Salt and freshly ground black pepper
To make the rolls:	To make the rolls:
450 g smoked salmon, thinly sliced	1 lb smoked salmon thinly sliced
429 g can asparagus spears, drained	15 oz can asparagus spears, drained
To garnish:	To garnish:
Lemon wedges	Lemon wedges

Smoked salmon wrapped around asparagus in horseradish cream is a luxurious starter for a wedding buffet. To make the horseradish cream: whip the cream until thick, then beat in the horseradish, wine vinegar, and salt and pepper to taste.

Cut the salmon into pieces approximately 7·5 cm (3 in) square and cut each asparagus spear in half. Lay the salmon pieces flat on a board, place one piece of asparagus in the centre of each piece of salmon, spoon a little of the horseradish cream over the asparagus and roll up the salmon neatly. Arrange on a serving platter and garnish with lemon wedges.

Makes about 34

Madras prawns

Madras prawns

Metric	Imperial
2 × 15 ml spoons vegetable oil	*2 tablespoons vegetable oil*
2 large onions, peeled and finely chopped	*2 large onions, peeled and finely chopped*
2 × 15 ml spoons garam masala or Madras curry powder, or to taste	*2 tablespoons garam masala or Madras curry powder, or to taste*
450 g peeled prawns	*1 lb peeled prawns*
Salt and freshly ground black pepper	*Salt and freshly ground black pepper*
200 g can tuna fish, drained and flaked	*7 oz can tuna fish, drained and flaked*
300 ml thick homemade mayonnaise (see page 20)	*½ pint thick homemade mayonnaise (see page 20)*
150 ml soured cream	*¼ pint soured cream*
1 × 15 ml spoon lemon juice	*1 tablespoon lemon juice*
1 kg long-grain rice, boiled, drained and rinsed	*2 lb long-grain rice, boiled, drained and rinsed*
4–5 × 15 ml spoons well seasoned vinaigrette dressing	*4–5 tablespoons well seasoned vinaigrette dressing*

To garnish:
1 large cucumber, peeled and thinly sliced
2 × 15 ml spoons finely chopped mint

To garnish:
1 large cucumber, peeled and thinly sliced
2 tablespoons finely chopped mint

This quantity makes two 23 cm (9 in) rice rings with a filling of prawns and tuna in a curried mayonnaise, and it is enough to serve approximately 25 persons as a starter. If you wish to make only one rice ring, then halve all the quantities given above. Serve with chilled dry white wine for a refreshing start to a buffet party meal.
Heat the oil in a large frying pan, add the onion and fry until soft and golden. Stir in the curry powder and cook for a further 2 minutes, stirring occasionally. Stir in the prawns, with salt and pepper to taste, and heat through. Remove the pan from the heat, transfer curried prawns to a mixing bowl and fold in the flaked tuna, mayonnaise, soured cream and lemon juice. Taste and adjust seasoning, then chill in the refrigerator until serving time. In a separate bowl, mix the rice with enough vinaigrette dressing to hold it together, then press into two oiled 23 cm (9 in) ring moulds. *Note:* if you only have one ring mould, make one rice ring, refrigerate and turn out, then oil the mould again and make the second rice ring. Chill in the refrigerator for at least 2 hours or overnight if possible. Turn the rice out on to serving platters and carefully spoon the prawn and tuna mixture into the centres, dividing it equally between the two. Arrange the cucumber slices on top of the rice and sprinkle the mint over the prawn and tuna filling.
Serves about 25

Smoked trout mousse

Smoked trout mousse

Metric

4 fresh smoked trout
(about 450 g), heads
removed, skinned, boned
and flaked
2 × 5 ml spoons lemon juice
150 ml mayonnaise (see
page 20)
150 ml double cream,
lightly whipped
¼ teaspoon cayenne pepper
Freshly ground white
pepper
1 × 15 ml spoon powdered
gelatine
2 × 15 ml spoons cold
water
2 egg whites

To garnish:
¼ cucumber, sliced
40 g jar lump fish roe
1 × 15 ml spoon aspic jelly
powder
150 ml water

Imperial

4 fresh smoked trout
(about 1 lb), heads
removed, skinned, boned
and flaked
2 teaspoons lemon juice
¼ pint mayonnaise (see
page 20)
¼ pint double cream,
lightly whipped
¼ teaspoon cayenne pepper
Freshly ground white
pepper
1 tablespoon powdered
gelatine
2 tablespoons cold
water
2 egg whites

To garnish:
¼ cucumber, sliced
1½ oz jar lump fish roe
1 tablespoon aspic jelly
powder
¼ pint water

Smooth and creamy, smoked trout mousse is deceptively rich and guests should be advised to help themselves to small portions. Serve with chilled dry white wine.

Put the smoked trout in a mixing bowl and sprinkle with the lemon juice. Add the mayonnaise and stir well to combine, then fold in the whipped cream. Season with the cayenne and white peppers.

Sprinkle the gelatine over the water in a small heatproof bowl and leave to stand until spongy. Put the bowl in a pan of hot water and stir over a low heat until the gelatine has dissolved.

Remove from the heat, leave to cool for 5 minutes, then stir into the trout mixture until evenly distributed. Chill in the refrigerator or leave in a cool place for approximately 1 hour until just beginning to set. Beat the egg whites until stiff, then fold into the mousse. Taste and adjust seasoning, then spoon into a 15 cm (6 in) soufflé dish, flatten top with a palette knife and chill in the refrigerator until set.

Decorate the top of mousse with the cucumber slices and lump fish roe. Make up the aspic jelly with the powder and water according to packet directions, leave to cool, then pour over the mousse. Return to the refrigerator and chill until serving time.

To freeze: wrap undecorated mousse in foil, overwrap in a freezer bag. Seal, label and freeze.

To thaw: unwrap and leave in the refrigerator overnight. Decorate after thawing.

Serves 12–14

33

Boned, stuffed and rolled chicken

Metric

1 roasting chicken (about
2½ kg), with the giblets
1 garlic clove, peeled and
cut in half
25 g butter, softened
Salt and freshly ground
black pepper

For the stuffing:
Butter for frying
1 large onion, peeled and
finely chopped
4 large sticks celery,
trimmed, scrubbed and
roughly chopped
225 g mushrooms, cleaned
and finely sliced
225 g back bacon, rinds
removed, chopped
100 g pork sausagemeat
Liver from chicken
giblets, chopped
100 g granary bread,
crumbled
50 g fresh parsley,
finely chopped
1 × 5 ml spoon mixed
dried herbs
Salt and freshly ground
black pepper
1 small egg, beaten
100 g stuffed green olives

To garnish:
Watercress sprigs

Imperial

1 roasting chicken (about
5 lb), with the giblets
1 garlic clove, peeled and
cut in half
1 oz butter, softened
Salt and freshly ground
black pepper

For the stuffing:
Butter for frying
1 large onion, peeled and
finely chopped
4 large sticks celery,
trimmed, scrubbed and
roughly chopped
8 oz mushrooms, cleaned
and finely sliced
8 oz back bacon, rinds
removed, chopped
4 oz pork sausagemeat
Liver from chicken
giblets, chopped
4 oz granary bread,
crumbled
2 oz fresh parsley,
finely chopped
1 teaspoon mixed
dried herbs
Salt and freshly ground
black pepper
1 small egg, beaten
4 oz stuffed green olives

To garnish:
Watercress sprigs

Cooking Time: About 2 hours
Oven: 190°C, 375°F, Gas Mark 5

Some butchers will bone a chicken for you; if not, then it is quite simple to bone it yourself by following the instructions given below, and it will be so much easier to carve the bird into neat slices at the buffet.

Remove the giblets from the chicken and reserve the liver for the stuffing. Wash the bird thoroughly and dry inside and out with a clean tea towel or absorbent kitchen paper. Put the bird on a working surface, breast side down. Slit the skin along the centre of the underside with a sharp knife, working from neck to tail end. Ease the flesh away from the carcass on one side of the bird, working down to the ball joint. Repeat this process on the other side.

Twist or cut off the scaly end of the leg, then cut through the legs where they join the carcass. Hold the leg bone and scrape the flesh away until the bones come free. Repeat with the other leg and the wings.

Continue to scrape the flesh away from the carcass on both sides, working round to the breastbone. When the breastbone is reached, carefully remove the flesh, being careful not to cut through the skin which is very thin at this point. Lift out the carcass. Lay the chicken as flat as possible on a board, skin side down. Rub the exposed flesh with the garlic clove and season.

To make the stuffing: melt a little butter in a pan, add the onion and celery and cook gently for approximately 5 minutes until soft and lightly coloured. Add the mushrooms and continue cooking for a further 2 to 3 minutes until the juices flow. Remove the vegetables from the pan with a slotted spoon and set aside in a mixing bowl. Add the bacon, sausagemeat and reserved chicken livers to the pan and cook for 5 minutes or until golden brown. Remove from the pan with a slotted spoon and add to the vegetables in the bowl. Stir in the crumbled bread, parsley and mixed herbs, with plenty of salt and pepper, mix well then bind the mixture with the egg.

Spread half the stuffing on the chicken, place the stuffed olives in a layer on top, then cover with the remaining stuffing. Roll up and tuck in the legs and wings. Overlap the skin on the underside and sew the bird neatly together with trussing string. Weigh the bird and calculate the cooking time, allowing 25 minutes to the ½ kg/1 lb. Place on a rack in a roasting tin. Rub the skin with the garlic clove, then brush with the softened butter and season. Roast in a fairly hot oven for about 1¾ hours, according to weight. Baste and turn occasionally during cooking.

Remove from the oven, leave to cool on the rack, then chill in the refrigerator until firm. Remove the trussing strings, slice the chicken neatly and transfer to a large serving platter. Garnish with sprigs of watercress. Alternatively, the whole chicken may be placed on a serving platter with just a few slices cut.

To freeze: wrap individual slices of chicken in cling film or foil, then pack together in a freezer bag. Seal, label and freeze.

To thaw: leave in wrappings in the refrigerator overnight.

Cuts into about 12 slices

Boned, stuffed and rolled chicken

Koulibiac

Metric	Imperial
700 g fresh salmon	*1½ lb fresh salmon*
300 ml dry white wine	*½ pint dry white wine*
1 bay leaf, crushed	*1 bay leaf, crushed*
1 large parsley sprig	*1 large parsley sprig*
4 black peppercorns	*4 black peppercorns*
Salt	*Salt*
50 g butter	*2 oz butter*
1 large onion, peeled and finely chopped	*1 large onion, peeled and finely chopped*
350 g button mushrooms, cleaned and finely sliced	*12 oz button mushrooms, cleaned and finely sliced*
225 g long-grain rice, boiled and drained	*8 oz long-grain rice, boiled and drained*
Finely grated rind and juice of 1 lemon	*Finely grated rind and juice of 1 lemon*
3 × 15 ml spoons finely chopped parsley	*3 tablespoons finely chopped parsley*
Freshly ground black pepper	*Freshly ground black pepper*
2 × 368 g packets frozen puff pastry, thawed	*2 × 13 oz packets frozen puff pastry, thawed*
3 hard-boiled eggs, shelled and sliced	*3 hard-boiled eggs, shelled and sliced*
1 egg, beaten	*1 egg, beaten*

To serve:
2 cartons soured cream

To serve:
2 cartons soured cream

Cooking Time: 1 hour 10 minutes
Oven: 200°C, 400°F, Gas Mark 6

This version of a classic Russian speciality makes a splendid centrepiece for a buffet party table, and is well worth the expense of the fresh salmon.

Put the salmon in a fish kettle or large saucepan, pour in the wine and enough water to cover the fish, then add the bay leaf, parsley sprig, peppercorns and salt to taste. Bring slowly to the boil, then lower the heat, cover with a lid and poach gently for approximately 20 minutes until the fish flakes easily with a fork. Remove the salmon from the kettle or pan, leave until cool enough to handle, discard any skin and bones, then flake the fish. Set aside.

Melt the butter in a pan, add the onion and cook gently until soft and lightly coloured. Add the mushrooms and cook for a further 2 minutes. Transfer this mixture to a mixing bowl, add the rice, lemon rind and juice, parsley and salt and pepper to taste. Mix gently.

Divide the dough into two portions, one slightly larger than the other. Roll out the smaller portion thinly on a floured board, transfer to a dampened baking sheet and cut into the shape of a fish, approximately 40 cm (16 in) long and 25 cm (10 in) at its widest point.

Divide the rice and mushroom mixture into two and spread one half on the dough, leaving a 2·5 cm (1 in) margin all round. Divide the salmon in two and lay half on top of the rice. Arrange the sliced hard-boiled eggs in a line down the centre of the salmon, then cover with a second layer of salmon and remaining rice mixture.

Roll out the larger piece of dough on a floured board and cut into the same shape as the first piece, but slightly larger. Lay the dough over the filling, seal the edges with a little water and flute them with the fingers or a fork. Brush all over with the beaten egg, make slits in the top to let the steam escape, then bake in a fairly hot oven for approximately 45 minutes until the pastry is golden brown. Remove from the oven, transfer to a serving platter and serve warm or cold. Pour the soured cream into a serving jug and hand separately.

To freeze: leave until completely cold, then open freeze until solid and wrap in foil or a large freezer bag. Store in the freezer for 1 to 2 days only.

To thaw: unwrap, place on a serving platter and leave at room temperature overnight.

Serves 10–12

Haricot bean salad

Metric	Imperial
1 kg dried haricot beans, soaked overnight	2 lb dried haricot beans, soaked overnight
2 large onions, peeled and very finely chopped	2 large onions, peeled and very finely chopped
2 large green peppers, cored, deseeded and finely diced	2 large green peppers, cored, deseeded and finely diced
2 large red peppers, cored, deseeded and finely diced	2 large red peppers, cored, deseeded and finely diced
225 g button mushrooms, cleaned and finely sliced	8 oz button mushrooms, cleaned and finely sliced

For the dressing:	For the dressing:
150 ml salad oil	$\frac{1}{4}$ pint salad oil
4 × 15 ml spoons tarragon vinegar	4 tablespoons tarragon vinegar
$\frac{1}{4}$ teaspoon sugar	$\frac{1}{4}$ teaspoon sugar
$\frac{1}{4}$ teaspoon English mustard powder	$\frac{1}{4}$ teaspoon English mustard powder
4 × 15 ml spoons finely chopped parsley	4 tablespoons finely chopped parsley
Salt and freshly ground black pepper	Salt and freshly ground black pepper

Drain the haricot beans and rinse under cold running water. Put in a large saucepan with plenty of water (without salt), bring to the boil, then lower the heat, half cover with a lid and simmer gently for 1 hour until tender. Check the water level from time to time during cooking and add more boiling water if it is low.

When the beans are cooked, drain and rinse under cold running water until cold. Turn into a large serving bowl, add the onions, peppers and mushrooms and stir well.

Pour the oil and vinegar into the bowl, add the remaining dressing ingredients with plenty of salt and pepper and toss the salad until the dressing coats the beans and vegetables. Chill in the refrigerator until serving time, toss well just before serving and adjust seasoning.

Serves about 25

Bean, sweetcorn and potato salad

Metric	Imperial
450 g packet frozen cut green beans	1 lb packet frozen cut green beans
2 × 225 g packets frozen sweetcorn and peppers	2 × 8 oz packets frozen sweetcorn and peppers
Salt	Salt
1 kg small new potatoes, scrubbed; or 2 × 538 g cans new potatoes	2 lb small new potatoes, scrubbed; or 2 × 1 lb 3 oz cans new potatoes
2 bunches of spring onions, trimmed, washed and roughly chopped	2 bunches of spring onions, trimmed, washed and roughly chopped
About 175 ml thick homemade mayonnaise (see page 20)	About 8 fl oz thick homemade mayonnaise (see page 20)
1 × 15 ml spoon lemon juice	1 tablespoon lemon juice
Freshly ground black pepper	Freshly ground black pepper

To garnish:	To garnish:
2 × 15 ml spoons finely chopped mint	2 tablespoons finely chopped mint

Cook the beans and sweetcorn in salted water according to packet directions, drain, rinse under cold running water and leave to cool. Meanwhile, boil the potatoes for approximately 15 minutes or until just barely tender. Drain, leave to cool for a few minutes, then remove any remaining skin, if liked. Leave to cool completely. (If using canned potatoes, drain, rinse under cold running water and drain again.) Slice thickly or cut into chunks.

Put the beans, sweetcorn and potatoes in a large mixing bowl with the spring onions and fold in the mayonnaise to coat the vegetables completely. Add the lemon juice, and salt and black pepper to taste, then turn the salad into a serving bowl and chill in the refrigerator. Sprinkle with the mint just before serving.

Serves about 15

Neapolitan salad; Haricot bean salad; Bean, sweetcorn and potato salad

Neapolitan salad

Metric

3 large bunches of
watercress, trimmed and
washed
2 large heads of fennel,
trimmed and finely
sliced
1½ kg firm ripe tomatoes,
quartered
2 large cucumbers, peeled,
seeded and cut into
julienne strips
2 × 50 g cans anchovies
4 hard-boiled eggs,
quartered
100 g black olives,
halved, stoned and
quartered

For the dressing:
2 × 15 ml spoons Meaux
mustard
3 × 15 ml spoons boiling
water
150 ml olive or salad oil
2 × 15 ml spoons lemon
juice
Salt and freshly ground
black pepper

Imperial

3 large bunches of
watercress, trimmed and
washed
2 large heads of fennel,
trimmed and finely
sliced
3 lb firm ripe tomatoes,
quartered
2 large cucumbers, peeled,
seeded and cut into
julienne strips
2 × 2 oz cans anchovies
4 hard-boiled eggs,
quartered
4 oz black olives,
halved, stoned and
quartered

For the dressing:
2 tablespoons Meaux
mustard
3 tablespoons boiling
water
¼ pint olive or salad oil
2 tablespoons lemon
juice
Salt and freshly ground
black pepper

This is an unusual variation of the classic Salad Niçoise. Put the watercress in a large serving bowl, add the fennel, tomatoes and cucumber and mix all the vegetables together with salad servers.

Soak the anchovies in milk for 30 minutes, drain, dry with absorbent kitchen paper and cut each one in half. Add to the salad bowl with the eggs and olives.

To make the dressing: put the mustard in a heatproof bowl and gradually beat in the boiling water. Add the oil drop by drop, beating constantly until the dressing is thick. Beat in the lemon juice and season to taste with salt and pepper.

Add the dressing to the salad bowl just before serving and toss well. Taste and adjust seasoning.

Serves about 20

Parmesan ham

Parmesan ham

Metric	Imperial
1×3 kg joint of gammon on the bone	1×6 lb joint of gammon on the bone
$\frac{1}{2}$ teaspoon ground mixed spice	$\frac{1}{2}$ teaspoon ground mixed spice
6 cloves	6 cloves
2 bay leaves	2 bay leaves
2×15 ml spoons wine vinegar	2 tablespoons wine vinegar
$2-3 \times 15$ ml spoons redcurrant jelly	2-3 tablespoons redcurrant jelly
50-75 g dried breadcrumbs	2-3 oz dried breadcrumbs
50-75 g Parmesan cheese, grated	2-3 oz Parmesan cheese, grated
Freshly ground black pepper	Freshly ground black pepper
100 g butter	4 oz butter

To garnish:
Few rings of fresh or canned pineapple

To garnish:
Few rings of fresh or canned pineapple

Cooking Time: $2\frac{1}{2}$–3 hours
Oven: 190°C, 375°F, Gas Mark 5

Soak the gammon in several changes of cold water for a minimum of 12 hours, then rinse under cold running water. Tie the joint securely with string. Put in a saucepan, cover with cold water and add the mixed spice, cloves, bay leaves and wine vinegar. Bring to the boil, skim the scum with a slotted spoon, then lower the heat, half cover with a lid and simmer gently for 2 to $2\frac{1}{2}$ hours until the ham is tender when pierced in the centre with a skewer.

Remove from the pan, leave until cold, then remove the string and cut off the rind, leaving a thin layer of fat. Brush this surface of the ham with redcurrant jelly. Mix the breadcrumbs and Parmesan cheese together, add black pepper to taste, then sprinkle and press this mixture on to the redcurrant jelly to cover it completely. Place the ham in a roasting pan with the butter and bake in a fairly hot oven for 30 to 40 minutes until the coating is golden brown, basting the ham occasionally with the butter. Remove from the pan and leave until completely cold. Cut a few slices from the ham and arrange with the whole ham on a carving board or platter, garnished with rings of pineapple.
Serves 12–15

Old fashioned English trifle

Old fashioned English trifle

Metric

8 trifle sponge cakes, cut
in half lengthwise
8 × 15 ml spoons red jam
8 × 15 ml spoons sherry
135 g packet jelly
4 fresh peaches, skinned,
halved and stoned
25 g demerara sugar, or to
taste
½ teaspoon ground
cinnamon
600 ml cold thick custard
300 ml whipping cream

To decorate:
25 g glacé cherries,
halved
Few strips of angelica
25 g blanched almonds,
split or flaked

Imperial

8 trifle sponge cakes, cut
in half lengthwise
8 tablespoons red jam
8 tablespoons sherry
4¾ oz packet jelly
4 fresh peaches, skinned,
halved and stoned
1 oz demerara sugar, or to
taste
½ teaspoon ground
cinnamon
1 pint cold thick custard
½ pint whipping cream

To decorate:
1 oz glacé cherries,
halved
Few strips of angelica
1 oz blanched almonds,
split or flaked

This trifle is best made with fresh peaches when in
season, but if unavailable, use canned peach halves.
Spread the insides of the sponge cakes with jam, then
sandwich them together again. Put in the bottom of a
large, deep trifle dish or glass fruit bowl, pour over the
sherry and leave to soak into the sponge.
Make the jelly according to packet directions, leave
until quite cold, then pour over the sponge cakes. Chill
in the refrigerator until set. Arrange the peach halves,
cut side down, on top of the jelly. Mix the sugar and
cinnamon together and sprinkle over the peaches. Spoon
the custard over to make an even layer, then chill in the
refrigerator until set.
Whip the cream until thick and spread over the custard,
swirling it with a knife. Decorate the top of trifle, making
flowers with cherry 'blooms' and angelica 'leaves'.
Arrange almonds decoratively between the flowers.
Chill in the refrigerator until serving time.
Serves 12–15

Tarte francaise

Metric	Imperial
For 300 g flan pastry (page 80)	For 10 oz flan pastry (page 80)

For the filling:
225 g sugar
600 ml water
1 kg fresh apricots, halved and stoned
175 g lemon curd
300 ml double cream
2 × 15 ml spoons arrowroot
2 × 15 ml spoons rum, lemon juice or water
4 × 15 ml spoons sieved apricot jam

For the filling:
8 oz sugar
1 pint water
2 lb fresh apricots, halved and stoned
6 oz lemon curd
½ pint double cream
2 tablespoons arrowroot
2 tablespoons rum, lemon juice or water
4 tablespoons sieved apricot jam

Cooking Time: 45 minutes
Oven: 190°C, 375°F, Gas Mark 5

Make the pastry and chill in the refrigerator for at least 1 hour.
For filling: heat sugar and water gently until the sugar has dissolved, then boil rapidly for 5 minutes. Lower the heat, add half the apricots, simmer gently for 5 minutes until tender but still whole. Remove with a slotted spoon and drain. Repeat with remaining apricots. Strain syrup and reserve. Press the chilled dough into a 30 cm (12 in) fluted flan tin with removable base. Chill for 30 minutes, then prick the base with a fork, cover with foil and fill with baking beans. Place on a baking sheet, in a fairly hot oven for 15 minutes, then remove foil and beans and bake a further 15 minutes until set and golden, remove leave to cool.
Spread the lemon curd over the base. Whip cream, then spread over the lemon curd. Arrange the drained apricot halves on top of the cream.
Mix the arrowroot with the rum, lemon juice or water. Return the sugar syrup to the heat, stir in arrowroot mixture and jam, then bring to the boil and simmer until thick. Remove from the heat, leave to cool slightly, then pour over the apricot.
Leave until set before serving.
Cut into about 12 portions.

Raspberry charlotte

Metric	Imperial

135 g packet raspberry jelly
450 g fresh or frozen raspberries, thawed
24 sponge fingers
100 g caster sugar
4 × 5 ml spoons powdered gelatine
2 × 15 ml spoons lemon juice
2 × 15 ml spoons water
450 ml fresh double cream
3 egg whites

4¾ oz packet raspberry jelly
1 lb fresh or frozen raspberries, thawed
24 sponge fingers
4 oz caster sugar
4 teaspoons powdered gelatine
2 tablespoons lemon juice
2 tablespoons water
¾ pint fresh double cream
3 egg whites

Make up the jelly with 300 ml (½ pint) water. Leave until beginning to set, then spoon half into a 20 cm (8 in) charlotte mould. Arrange some raspberries on top of the jelly and sprinkle with a little sugar. Brush sides of sponge fingers with some jelly, then line the mould with the fingers by standing them upright in the jelly closely together. Spoon any remaining jelly into the mould. Chill until set. Meanwhile, put the remaining raspberries and sugar in a saucepan and heat gently for 5 minutes or until soft. Leave to cool, purée in a blender, then sieve.
Sprinkle the gelatine over lemon juice and water in a bowl and leave to stand until spongy. Put the bowl over a pan of hot water and stir over low heat until dissolved. Leave to cool slightly, then stir into the raspberry purée. Leave until just beginning to thicken. Whip cream until thick, then fold into the purée, reserving some for decoration. Beat egg whites until stiff and fold these in. When jelly has set in mould spoon in the raspberry cream. Trim ends of sponge fingers, cover with foil or a plate and chill in refrigerator for several hours.
Note: if the charlotte is difficult to unmould, dip the base of the mould very quickly in a bowl of hot water.
To freeze: freeze in the mould or tin. Cover with foil, overwrap in a freezer bag. Seal, label and freeze.
To thaw: unwrap, unmould onto a serving plate and leave for 4 hours at room temperature.
Three Raspberry charlottes serve 10–12

Tarte francaise; Raspberry charlotte

2-tier iced wedding cake

This two-tier wedding cake has a delicately pretty design of bunches of grapes and trellis work. The bottom tier will cut into 80 pieces and the top tier into 50 pieces.

Follow the instructions for the Anniversary Cake (page 26), baking the rich fruit mixture in a 25 cm (10 in) round cake tin–this will form the bottom tier of the cake. Make a 15 cm (6 in) round rich fruit cake using one third of the mixture for the Anniversary Cake–this will form the top tier of the cake. Leave both cakes to mature for one month, spooning over more spirits from time to time. Make the almond paste as in the recipe below and use to coat the 25 cm (10 in) cake. Make a second batch, using one third of the ingredients, and use to coat the 15 cm (6 in) cake. Leave both cakes to dry out for one week.

To decorate the cake:

1. Make up the same quantity of royal icing as for the Anniversary Cake, (without food colouring), and use to coat the large cake. Prick air bubbles. Quickly scoop up the surplus icing and use to coat the small cake; prick air bubbles. Scoop up any remaining icing, put in a bowl and cover with a lid or damp cloth. Leave both cakes and surplus icing overnight.

2. The next day, lift the large cake on to a 30 cm (12 in) round silver cake board and the small cake on to a 20 cm (8 in) round silver cake board. Make up a batch of royal icing using 1 egg white, 225 g (8 oz) sieved icing sugar and 1×5 ml spoon (1 teaspoon) glycerine. Thicken the surplus icing from coating the cakes with more icing sugar until the same consistency as the freshly made batch then mix the two batches together.

3. Fit a piping bag with a No. 4 plain tube, put in some of the icing and pipe a large smooth beading around the base of each cake to neaten it and join it to the boards.

4. Fit a piping bag with a No. 2 plain tube, put in some of the icing and pipe small dots in between the beading, one row of dots on the cakes and one row on the boards.

5. Using the No. 2 plain tube, mark eight tiny dots around the side of the large cake, just below the edge. Space them evenly apart, using a marking ring or greaseproof paper folded into eight. Repeat with the small cake, marking four dots around the side.

6. Take a plain biscuit cutter or glass with a diameter of 5 cm (2 in) and pipe dots of icing around the edge or rim. Press on to the sides of the cake beneath the tiny dots already marked–the dots will adhere to the cake to form circles. Make eight circles on the large cake, four on the small.

7. Using the No. 2 plain tube, pipe parallel diagonal lines across each circle, approximately 6 mm ($\frac{1}{4}$ in) apart. Repeat these lines in the opposite direction, then over-pipe both ways to form a trellis. Pipe a small beading around each circle to neaten the edge.

8. Using the No. 2 plain tube, pipe three rough triangles upside-down in between each circle, one large triangle in the centre with two smaller ones at each side. Working from the bottom upwards, pipe a small beading all over the triangles to resemble bunches of grapes. Pipe stems to join the bunches of grapes.

9. Make a plain greaseproof paper cone and cut a tiny hole at the end. Put some icing into the cone and pipe random tendrils around the bunches of grapes. Cut the end of the cone to make a leaf point, squeeze out a little icing on a tendril and pull away, releasing the pressure to make a vine leaf. Repeat on all the tendrils.

10. Put four 6 cm ($2\frac{1}{2}$ in) white pillars on the large cake and stand the small cake on top. Decorate the top of the cake with an ornament or small vase of flowers.

Note: for a three-tier cake, make the middle tier with half the rich fruit cake mixture used in the 25 cm (10 in) cake and bake in a 20 cm (8 in) round cake tin. Make half the quantity of almond paste and one and a half times the quantity of royal icing.

Almond paste

Metric	Imperial
350 g ground almonds	*12 oz ground almonds*
175 g caster sugar	*6 oz caster sugar*
175 g icing sugar, sieved	*6 oz icing sugar, sieved*
1 egg	*1 egg*
3 egg yolks	*3 egg yolks*
1–2 × 15 ml spoons lemon juice	*1–2 tablespoons lemon juice*
Few drops of almond or vanilla essence (optional)	*Few drops of almond or vanilla essence (optional)*
About 3 × 15 ml spoons sieved apricot jam, warmed	*About 3 tablespoons sieved apricot jam, warmed*

Put the almonds and sugars in a bowl and mix well. Beat the egg and egg yolks together with half the lemon juice, and the essence if using. Add to the almond mixture and mix carefully until the paste comes together, adding more lemon juice if necessary. Do not overwork.

Brush the top of the cake with apricot jam. Halve almond paste and roll out one piece on a board sprinkled with icing sugar, to a round slightly larger than the cake. Lift on to the rolling pin and lay over the cake. Trim.

Brush the sides of the cake with the remaining jam. Roll out the remaining paste into a rectangle, long enough to go half round cake and twice as deep; cut into two. Press one piece at a time on to the cake, cutting away any excess along the top. Smooth the joins with a palette knife, smooth the top of the cake with a rolling pin and roll a straight-sided jar round the sides. Leave to dry for at least one week before icing.

Long summer evenings lend themselves perfectly to
garden barbecue parties. Entertaining is simple and fun,
the cooking being shared between hostess and guests.
Most barbecue dishes are simply marinated and then
cooked over charcoal—this gives them the
characteristic smoky barbecue flavour. There is therefore
very little cooking or preparation to be done before guests arrive.
Whether you have sophisticated barbecue equipment or a
do-it-yourself arrangement made from a few bricks and a
grid, barbecue cooking could not be easier. To be
successful, the charcoal must be very hot before the
food is placed on the grid, and the coals should burn
for about 30 minutes so that the flames die down and the
charcoal becomes grey. The grid should be placed on the
charcoals from the beginning so that it is very hot when
fish, meat or poultry is first placed on it.
Always baste the food well while it is cooking.

Hummus

Metric

350 g dried chick peas,
soaked overnight
2–3 garlic cloves,
according to taste, peeled
1 × 5 ml spoon salt
About 150 ml lemon juice
About 150 ml hot water
About 150 ml tahini
paste
2–3 × 15 ml spoons olive
oil

To garnish:
2 × 15 ml spoons finely
chopped mint or parsley

Imperial

12 oz dried chick peas,
soaked overnight
2–3 garlic cloves,
according to taste, peeled
1 teaspoon salt
About ¼ pint lemon juice
About ¼ pint hot water
About ¼ pint tahini
paste
2–3 tablespoons olive
oil

To garnish:
2 tablespoons finely
chopped mint or parsley

Cooking Time: 1 hour

Serve this Middle Eastern dip with hot flat Greek or Arab bread known as pita, or, if this is unavailable, substitute crisp French bread. Tahini paste is available at most Middle Eastern shops and health food stores.

Drain the chick peas and rinse thoroughly under cold running water. Put in a large saucepan with plenty of cold water, bring to the boil, then lower the heat, half cover with a lid and simmer for approximately 1 hour or until the chick peas are tender. Drain, rinse under cold running water and set aside.

Crush the garlic cloves with the salt and put in an electric blender with some of the chick peas, lemon juice, hot water and tahini paste. Blend at high speed until a smooth purée is obtained. Repeat this blending process until all the chick peas have been puréed, adding more tahini paste, lemon juice and hot water to obtain a smooth, creamy consistency.

Transfer to a bowl, beat well with a wooden spoon and adjust the consistency of the hummus with more lemon juice or hot water if it is too thick. Taste and add more salt if necessary.

Pour hummus into a shallow serving bowl, spoon over the olive oil and sprinkle with mint or parsley.

Refrigerate until serving time.

To freeze: leave in the serving bowl without oil and mint or parsley, or transfer to a rigid container. Cover with foil, wrap in a freezer bag, then overwrap. Seal, label and freeze.

To thaw: leave in wrappings in refrigerator overnight, then unwrap and finish with oil and mint or parsley before serving.

Serves 10

Hummus; Lebanese cucumber soup

Lebanese cucumber soup

Metric

2 large cucumbers, peeled
Salt
Pinch of sugar
2 garlic cloves, peeled and
crushed with ½ teaspoon salt
1 l natural yogurt
2 × 5 ml spoons lemon
juice
3 × 15 ml spoons finely
chopped mint
Freshly ground black
pepper

Imperial

2 large cucumbers, peeled
Salt
Pinch of sugar
2 garlic cloves, peeled and
crushed with ½ teaspoon salt
2 pints natural yogurt
2 teaspoons lemon
juice
3 tablespoons finely
chopped mint
Freshly ground black
pepper

If possible, try to use live Balkan-type yogurt for this uncooked soup. It is normally available from health food shops and its thin consistency makes it the most suitable kind for making soup.

Grate the cucumbers coarsely, place in a sieve, sprinkle with salt and leave to drain for 30 minutes. Transfer to a chilled soup tureen or large serving bowl, add the sugar and stir in the garlic. Gradually pour in the yogurt, stirring constantly, then stir in the lemon juice, two-thirds of the mint, and pepper to taste. Taste and adjust seasoning, then sprinkle over the remaining mint and grind a little pepper over the soup to finish.

Chill in the refrigerator until serving time.

Serves 8–10

Tandoori chicken

Metric

2 × 5 cm pieces fresh
root ginger, peeled
and chopped
3 garlic cloves, peeled
and chopped
3 black peppercorns
2 × 5 ml spoons chilli
powder
2 × 5 ml spoons ground
coriander seeds
1 × 5 ml spoon ground
cumin seeds
½ teaspoon salt
Finely grated rind and
juice of 1 lemon
1–2 drops of bright red
food colouring
10 chicken breasts or
drumsticks, skinned
10 × 15 ml spoons natural
yogurt

To finish:
1–2 lettuces, washed and
separated into leaves
3 tomatoes, quartered
1 cucumber, sliced
Salt and freshly ground
black pepper

Imperial

2 × 2 in pieces fresh
root ginger, peeled
and chopped
3 garlic cloves, peeled
and chopped
3 black peppercorns
2 teaspoon chilli
powder
2 teaspoons ground
coriander seeds
1 teaspoon ground
cumin seeds
½ teaspoon salt
Finely grated rind and
juice of 1 lemon
1–2 drops of bright red
food colouring
10 chicken breasts or
drumsticks, skinned
10 tablespoons natural
yogurt

To finish:
1–2 lettuces, washed and
separated into leaves
3 tomatoes, quartered
1 cucumber, sliced
Salt and freshly ground
black pepper

Cooking Time: 20 minutes

This dish owes its name to the traditional clay oven in which it is cooked – the tandoor. Cooking on a barbecue makes a very acceptable substitute as the charcoal helps to give the chicken an authentic flavour.

Pound the root ginger, garlic and peppercorns in a pestle and mortar. Mix with the chilli powder, ground coriander and cumin, salt, lemon rind and juice and food colouring. Score the chicken flesh with the point of a very sharp knife, then rub the pounded mixture into the skin. Brush each chicken portion with 1 × 15 ml spoon (1 tablespoon) yogurt, then chill in the refrigerator for 24 hours. Let stand at room temperature for 1 to 2 hours before cooking.

When the barbecue charcoals are hot, place the chicken on the grid and cook for approximately 20 minutes until the outside of the chicken is charred and the meat is cooked through, turning the portions frequently.

Arrange lettuce leaves, tomato quarters and slices of cucumber on a serving platter and sprinkle liberally with salt and pepper. Place tandoori chicken on top of salad; serve immediately with yogurt handed separately.
Serves 10

Tandoori chicken

Sweet and sour pork kebabs

Metric

About 1½ kg pork
(tenderloin), fillet
cut into cubes
Salt and freshly ground
black pepper

For the marinade:
6 × 15 ml spoons
vegetable oil
Finely grated rind and
juice of 1½ grapefruits
3 × 15 ml spoons dark
soft brown sugar
3 × 15 ml spoons soy
sauce
2 × 15 ml spoons black
treacle
3 fresh green chillis,
finely chopped
1 × 5 cm piece fresh
root ginger, peeled,
chopped and pounded to
a paste
mortar
1 × 5 ml spoon Tabasco
sauce

To serve:
Natural yogurt

Imperial

About 3 lb pork
(tenderloin), fillet
cut into cubes
Salt and freshly ground
black pepper

For the marinade:
6 tablespoons
vegetable oil
Finely grated rind and
juice of 1½ grapefruits
3 tablespoons dark
soft brown sugar
3 tablespoons soy
sauce
2 tablespoons black
treacle
3 fresh green chillis,
finely chopped
1 × 2 in piece fresh
root ginger, peeled,
chopped and pounded to
a paste
mortar
1 teaspoon Tabasco
sauce

To serve:
Natural yogurt

Cooking Time: 15 minutes

These hot spicy kebabs should be served with chilled ratatouille and jacket potatoes, or hot French bread and a tossed green salad.

Put the pork in a large bowl and sprinkle liberally with salt and pepper. Mix all the ingredients for the marinade together, beating briskly to combine thoroughly. Pour over the pork and stir well so that each cube of meat is coated in the marinade. Chill in the refrigerator for 24 hours, stirring the meat and marinade together from time to time. Let stand at room temperature for 1 to 2 hours before cooking.

Thread the cubes of pork on to 8–10 oiled kebab skewers while the barbecue charcoals are heating. When they are hot, place the kebabs on the grid and cook for approximately 15 minutes, turning the skewers regularly and brushing the pork with the remaining marinade. Serve immediately with yogurt handed separately. Serves 8–10.

Sweet and sour pork kebabs

Sheftalia

Metric	Imperial
1¼ kg boned lean lamb	2½ lb boned lean lamb
1 large onion, peeled and chopped	1 large onion, peeled and chopped
2 garlic cloves, peeled and crushed with 1 × 5 ml spoon salt	2 garlic cloves, peeled and crushed with 1 teaspoon salt
6 × 15 ml spoons finely chopped parsley	6 tablespoons finely chopped parsley
1 small egg, beaten	1 small egg, beaten
1 × 5 ml spoon ground allspice	1 teaspoon ground allspice
Freshly ground black pepper	Freshly ground black pepper
Flour seasoned with salt and pepper for coating	Flour seasoned with salt and pepper for coating
Vegetable oil for cooking	Vegetable oil for cooking
Few fresh rosemary sprigs	Few fresh rosemary sprigs

Cooking Time: 10–15 minutes

These Greek-style kebabs combine minced lamb with onion and garlic. Serve them with yogurt and a tomato and onion salad sprinkled with plenty of finely chopped fresh coriander or parsley.

Mince the lamb, onion, garlic and parsley together several times until the mixture is fine and smooth. Stir in the egg and allspice and black pepper to taste and mix until evenly blended. Form the mixture into thin sausage shapes, approximately 6 cm (2½ in) long, and roll between well-floured hands until the kebabs are firm and lightly coated in flour. Chill in the refrigerator for 24 hours, then thread carefully on to oiled kebab skewers and brush gently with oil. When the barbecue charcoals are hot, put a few rosemary sprigs on the well-oiled barbecue grid. Place the kebabs on top and cook for 10 to 15 minutes, turning the kebabs during cooking, and brushing with more oil from time to time. Remove from the barbecue and serve hot as suggested above.

To freeze: open freeze uncooked sheftalia on trays until solid, then pack in freezer bags or rigid containers and overwrap. Seal, label and return to freezer.

To thaw: cook on the barbecue from frozen, allowing a few extra minutes cooking time until cooked through.

Makes about 40.

Chilled ratatouille

Metric	Imperial
2 large aubergines, sliced	2 large aubergines, sliced
Salt	Salt
Olive oil for frying	Olive oil for frying
2 large onions, peeled and finely sliced	2 large onions, peeled and finely sliced
2 garlic cloves, peeled and crushed	2 garlic cloves, peeled and crushed
2 large green or red peppers, cored, seeded and finely sliced	2 large green or red peppers, cored, seeded and finely sliced
700 g courgettes, sliced	1½ lb courgettes, sliced
700 g tomatoes, skinned, seeded and chopped	1½ lb tomatoes, skinned, seeded and chopped
2 × 15 ml spoons tomato purée	2 tablespoons tomato purée
½ teaspoon sugar	½ teaspoon sugar
Freshly ground black pepper	Freshly ground black pepper

This vegetable dish from the Provençe region of France is most often served hot, but it is especially good when served chilled as an accompaniment to hot, spicy barbecued meat and poultry.

Spread the aubergine slices in a single layer on a large plate or board and sprinkle liberally with salt. Leave to stand for 30 minutes, then rinse under cold running water and pat dry with absorbent kitchen paper. Heat 4 spoons of oil in a large saucepan. Add the onion and garlic and fry gently until soft and lightly coloured. Add the peppers and fry for a further 5 minutes, then add the aubergine slices, courgettes and tomatoes. Increase the heat and cook briskly for a few minutes, stirring constantly. Stir in the tomato purée, sugar and black pepper to taste, then lower the heat, cover with a lid and cook gently for approximately 40 minutes, or until the vegetables are soft. Remove from the heat, taste and adjust seasoning, and leave to cool. When cold, chill in the refrigerator until serving time.

Serves 10

Strawberry shortcake

Strawberry shortcake

Metric	Imperial
100 g butter	4 oz butter
75 g caster sugar	3 oz caster sugar
100 g roasted hazelnuts, finely ground	4 oz roasted hazelnuts, finely ground
175 g flour	6 oz flour
450 ml double or whipping cream	¾ pink double or whipping cream
50 g icing sugar	2 oz icing sugar
450 g strawberries, hulled and washed	1 lb strawberries, hulled and washed

Cooking Time: 15 to 20 minutes
Oven: 190°C, 375°F, Gas Mark 5

Assemble this cake just before serving time. Cream the butter and caster sugar together until light and fluffy, then beat in the hazelnuts and flour a little at a time. Form the mixture into three equal balls and chill in the refrigerator for at least 30 minutes until firm. With floured fingers, press each ball into a 20 cm (8 in) circle on parchment paper placed on a baking sheet, Cut one of the circles into eight triangles with a sharp knife. Bake in the centre of a fairly hot oven for 15 to 20 minutes or until golden brown (if necessary, bake each circle separately as the pastry will cook too quickly if not baked in the centre of the oven). Remove from the oven and cut through the eight triangles of the one circle to separate them. Leave the pastry for 5 to 10 minutes to cool slightly and become firm, then carefully ease off the parchment paper. Leave to cool. Whip the cream until thick with most of the icing sugar, reserving a little for dusting. Slice the strawberries, reserving four for decoration, and fold into the whipped cream.

Place one whole round of hazelnut pastry on a serving platter and spread with half the strawberry and cream mixture. Place the second round of pastry on top and spread with the remaining strawberries and cream. Arrange the eight 'triangles' on top of the cake, dust with icing sugar and decorate each with a strawberry. Serves 8

Pineapple sorbet

Pineapple sorbet

Metric

1 ripe fresh pineapple
(about 1½ kg), cut in
half lengthwise
2 egg whites

For the sugar syrup:
100 g sugar
300 ml water

Imperial

1 ripe fresh pineapple
(about 3 lb), cut in
half lengthwise
2 egg whites

For the sugar syrup:
4 oz sugar
½ pint water

Cooking Time: 10–15 minutes

Nothing is more refreshing in hot weather than a tangy sorbet or water ice. If making in a domestic refrigerator, turn the thermostat to its coldest setting before preparing sorbet.

Scoop out the pineapple flesh and juice, reserving the pineapple shells, and purée in an electric blender. Transfer to a mixing bowl.

To make the sugar syrup: put sugar and water in a heavy-based saucepan and heat gently until the sugar has dissolved. Increase the heat and boil rapidly for 7 to 10 minutes until syrupy, then remove from the heat and leave until cold. Mix the pineapple purée and sugar syrup together, pour into a freezer tray and freeze in the ice box of the refrigerator or in the freezer. Leave until the mixture becomes mushy.

Turn the mixture into a bowl and beat with an electric or rotary beater. Beat the egg whites until stiff, then fold into the pineapple mixture. Spoon the mixture into the pineapple shells and return to the ice box or freezer.

Freeze for at least 2 hours or overnight. Transfer to main part of refrigerator 15 minutes before serving.

To freeze: wrap each pineapple half separately in cling film, then overwrap in a freezer bag. Seal, label and freeze. Unwrap before transferring to refrigerator before serving.

Serves 8

The most important thing to bear in mind when preparing food for a children's party is that the food must look attractive—children need their appetites stimulated when they are busy playing party games and enjoying themselves.
All the food in this birthday party menu can be prepared well in advance. The ice-cream and cakes can even be stored in the freezer if you have one, therefore there is no need to be frantically busy in the kitchen at a time when you should be organising—and joining in—all the fun.

Surprise thatched cottage

Metric	Imperial
1 large white or brown loaf	1 large white or brown loaf
450 g cocktail sausages, cooked	1 lb cocktail sausages, cooked
½ cucumber, sliced	½ cucumber, sliced
100 g cream cheese	4 oz cream cheese
About 75 g potato sticks	About 3 oz potato sticks
1 stick celery, trimmed and scrubbed	1 stick celery, trimmed and scrubbed
2 slices of processed cheese	2 slices of processed cheese

You can fill the bread 'cottage' with any titbits you think your children may like—cocktail sausages, crisps, cubes of cheese and pineapple, baby sausage rolls, miniature sandwiches, nuts, etc. For a small party, use a small loaf.

Cut the top off the loaf and reserve to make the roof. Scoop the bread from the inside of the loaf and fill the hollow with cocktail sausages. Place on a board or serving platter. Place the cucumber slices to form a thick layer on top of the loaf. Spread the roof thickly with cream cheese, reserving some for the chimney, windows and doors, then place on top of the cucumber slices.

Press the potato sticks into the cream cheese to form the thatch. Cut the celery stick in two, then cut in half lengthwise. Sandwich two of the halves together with cream cheese, press into the top of the house for the chimney, then add two potato sticks for the smoke.

Cut the cheese slices into squares to make windows for the front, back and sides of the cottage, and cut two oblong shapes to make front and back doors. Stick these shapes on to the loaf with a little cream cheese and use potato sticks to make frames for the windows, a knocker and letterbox for the front door. Use the remaining two pieces of celery to make a porch above the door.

Surprise thatched cottage

Chocolate crispies

Metric	Imperial
100 g milk chocolate, broken into squares	4 oz milk chocolate, broken into squares
2 × 15 ml spoons milk	2 tablespoons milk
2 × 15 ml spoons Golden Syrup	2 tablespoons Golden Syrup
100 g cornflakes, lightly crushed	4 oz cornflakes, lightly crushed
50 g desiccated coconut	2 oz desiccated coconut

Cooking Time: 5 minutes

Put the chocolate, milk and Golden Syrup into a heavy-based saucepan and heat gently until melted, stirring occasionally to mix the ingredients together. Put the cornflakes in a mixing bowl and stir in the chocolate mixture and the coconut. Stir to combine, then divide mixture equally between 12 to 14 paper bun cases. Chill in the refrigerator until set, then store in an airtight tin.
Makes 12–14

Jelly roll

Metric	Imperial
2 × 227 g cans pineapple rings	2 × 8 oz cans pineapple rings
135 g packet strawberry or raspberry jelly	4¾ oz packet strawberry or raspberry jelly
Few grapes, stalks removed and washed	Few grapes, stalks removed and washed

You can use a different-flavoured jelly if preferred, and substitute strawberries, raspberries, mandarin oranges or nuts for the grapes used here. You will need a large empty can to use as a mould–538 g (1 lb 3 oz) is the most suitable size and it can be kept for future use.
Drain the pineapple rings and measure the juice. Make the jelly according to packet directions, using the pineapple juice with the cold water.
Pour a little of the jelly into the rinsed-out can to just cover the bottom. Chill in the refrigerator until set. Place one pineapple ring carefully on top of the set jelly, put a grape in the centre, then pour over more jelly to cover and chill in the refrigerator until set. Continue making layers of jelly, pineapple and grapes until the can is full, chilling each layer of jelly until set before proceeding with the next layer. Chill in the refrigerator for 1 hour, then unmould on to a serving platter.
Cuts into 8 slices

Pear church mice

Metric	Imperial
822 g can pear halves	1 lb 13 oz can pear halves
2 × 135 g packets lime jelly	2 × 4¾ oz packets lime jelly
21 sultanas, raisins or currants	21 sultanas, raisins or currants
25 g angelica	1 oz angelica

Drain the pears and measure the juice. Make the jelly according to packet directions, using the pear juice with the water. Pour into a shallow tin or tray and chill in the refrigerator until set.
Chop the jelly roughly with a knife and arrange on a serving board or plate. Arrange the pear halves on the jelly, cut side down, then press in the dried fruit to make two eyes and one nose for each mouse. Cut the angelica into very fine strips and stick a few strips on either side of each nose to form whiskers. Chill in the refrigerator until serving time.
Makes 7

Butterfly cakes

Butterfly cakes

Metric

For the cakes:
*100 g butter or
margarine, softened
100 g caster sugar
2 eggs, beaten
75 g self-raising flour
Pinch of salt
25 g cocoa powder
1 × 15 ml spoon warm water*

For the butter icing:
*50 g butter
100 g icing sugar, sieved
2 × 15 ml spoons water
1 small packet chocolate
buttons*

To finish:
Chocolate vermicelli

Imperial

For the cakes:
*4 oz butter or
margarine, softened
4 oz caster sugar
2 eggs, beaten
3 oz self-raising flour
Pinch of salt
1 oz cocoa powder
1 tablespoon warm water*

For the butter icing:
*2 oz butter
4 oz icing sugar, sieved
2 tablespoons water
1 small packet chocolate
buttons*

To finish:
Chocolate vermicelli

Cooking Time: 15 minutes
Oven: 190°C, 375°F, Gas Mark 5

Although using only a simple cake mixture and a little butter icing, these pretty cakes never fail to attract children at a birthday party.

Cream the butter or margarine and sugar together until light and fluffy, then gradually beat in the eggs a little at a time. Sieve the flour, salt and cocoa powder together and gradually fold into the butter and sugar mixture. Beat in the warm water. Divide the mixture between 20 small paper cake cases and bake in a fairly hot oven for 15 minutes until risen and golden brown. Remove from the oven and leave to cool. Meanwhile, make the butter icing: beat the butter until soft, then gradually beat in the icing sugar a little at a time, adding 1 × 15 ml spoon (1 tablespoon) water when the mixture becomes too stiff to beat. Put the chocolate buttons and the water in to a small heavy-based saucepan and heat gently until melted, stirring occasionally. Beat the melted chocolate into the butter icing until evenly distributed.

Cut the tops off the cakes and cut in half. Put a blob of butter cream icing on top of each cake and press in the tops to form wings. Sprinkle each butterfly with chocolate vermicelli.

To freeze: open freeze until solid, then pack in single layers in rigid containers. Seal, label and freeze.

To thaw: remove from containers, transfer to a serving platter and leave at room temperature for 2 to 3 hours.
Makes 20

Iced cookies

Iced cookies

Metric	Imperial
225 g flour	8 oz flour
Pinch of salt	Pinch of salt
100 g sugar	4 oz sugar
125 g butter or margarine	4 oz butter or margarine
1 egg yolk	1 egg yolk
1–2 × 15 ml spoons cold water	1–2 tablespoons cold water

For the glacé icing:

Metric	Imperial
100 g icing sugar, sieved	4 oz icing sugar, sieved
1–2 × 15 ml spoons hot water	1–2 tablespoons hot water
Few drops each of bright red, yellow, green and blue food colourings	Few drops each of bright red, yellow, green and blue food colourings

Cooking Time: 10 minutes
Oven: 180°C, 350°F, Gas Mark 4

These cookies can be made in any shape you fancy—stars, rings, dogs, cats, etc., and it is now possible to buy sets of fancy cookie cutters at most good kitchen shops. Sift the flour and salt into a mixing bowl and stir in the sugar. Cut the butter or margarine into pieces and work into the flour and sugar with the fingertips. Stir in the egg and enough cold water to draw the mixture together. Form the dough into a ball, wrap in foil and chill in the refrigerator for at least 30 minutes. Roll out the chilled dough on a well-floured board and stamp into approximately 50 shapes with small fancy cookie cutters. Place on greased baking sheets and bake in a moderate oven for approximately 10 minutes until the cookies are set and golden. Remove from the oven and cool on a wire rack. Meanwhile, make the glacé icing: put the icing sugar in a bowl and gradually beat in the hot water, adding enough to let the icing coat the back of a spoon. Divide the icing into three or four and add different food colourings to each. Spread immediately on top of the biscuits, then leave to set. If liked, the round cookies can be made into faces with currants for eyes, halved glacé cherries for noses and a curved strip of orange or lemon rind for the mouth. Dogs and cats can also have faces made in this way. Star-shaped cookies can be decorated with silver dragees at each point. Add decorations immediately after icing, then leave to set. Store in an airtight tin.
Makes about 50

Numeral cakes

Metric

For the cake:
225 g butter or margarine,
softened
225 g caster sugar
4 eggs, beaten
225 g self-raising flour
Pinch of salt
2–3 × 15 ml spoons warm
water
3 × 15 ml spoons jam

For the icing:
150 g butter
350 g icing sugar, sieved
2 × 15 ml spoons hot water
Food colouring
Smarties or sugared roses
Candles

Imperial

For the cake:
8 oz butter or margarine,
softened
8 oz caster sugar
4 eggs, beaten
8 oz self-raising flour
Pinch of salt
2–3 tablespoons warm
water
3 tablespoons jam

For the icing:
5 oz butter
12 oz icing sugar, sieved
2 tablespoons hot water
Food colouring
Smarties or sugared roses
Candles

Cooking Time: 30 minutes
Oven: 190°C, 375°F, Gas Mark 5

The quantities given left are sufficient to make two cakes to form the number ten. If you are making one of the smaller numbers you will obviously have to trim to waste, but any trimmings can be used for making trifles, or simply eaten by the children!

Grease an 18 cm (7 in) ring mould and an 18 cm (7 in) square shallow cake tin. Prepare the cake mixture as in the recipe for Butterfly Cakes (see page 58) and divide the mixture between the two tins. Bake in a fairly hot oven for 30 minutes or until risen and golden brown. Remove from the oven, turn out on to a wire rack and leave to cool.

Cut the ring cake in half horizontally, spread one of the cut surfaces with some of the jam, then sandwich the two halves together again. Cut the square cake in half vertically, spread the top of one half with the remaining jam and sandwich the two halves together, one on top of the other.

To make the icing: beat butter until soft, then gradually beat in the icing sugar a little at a time, adding the water gradually as the mixture becomes too stiff to beat. Add a few drops of food colouring according to taste.

Spread the icing smoothly over the two cakes, then press Smarties or roses around the edges. Place candles on top of the cake and make the child's name with more Smarties or roses, if wished.

Instructions for making other numbers:

Two Half of one circular cake, plus one square cake cut and sandwiched together as above, then cut into two pieces, one slightly longer than the other. Trim to shape.

Three Half of one circular cake, plus one square cake cut and sandwiched together as above, then cut into two equal pieces. Trim at the joins and trim to shape.

Four Two square cakes, each one cut and sandwiched together as above. Cut 5 cm/2 in off each cake and use the four pieces to make the number.

Five Half of one circular cake, plus one square cake cut and sandwiched together as above, then cut into two pieces, one slightly longer than the other. Trim to shape.

Six One circular cake, plus one square cake cut and sandwiched together as above. Trim to shape at the join with the circle.

Seven Two square cakes, each one cut and sandwiched together as above. Trim at the join.

Eight Two circular cakes. Trim at the join.

Nine One circular cake, plus one square cake cut and sandwiched together as above. Trim to shape at the join with the circle.

To freeze: open freeze without decorations until solid, then wrap loosely in foil or a freezer bag. Seal, label and return to freezer.

To thaw: unwrap, place on a serving platter and leave for 3 to 4 hours at room temperature. Decorate after thawing.

* Numeral cake

Whether it is a romantic dinner for two on Valentine's
Day or a more formal party to entertain your husband's
business colleagues, you will want the food to be
something rather special. A dinner party is one of
the few occasions when it is permissible to be
extravagant and use the more unusual and luxurious
ingredients, and it is therefore one of the times
when the cook can really enjoy herself.
All the recipes suggested here are suitable for a celebration.
The first menu in this section serves two; the second serves six.

Goujons de sole with tartare sauce

Metric

2–3 small fillets lemon sole,
(about 350 g) skinned
and cut into 2·5 cm strips
2 × 15 ml spoons flour
Salt and freshly ground
black pepper
2 eggs, beaten
About 100 g dried
breadcrumbs
Oil for deep frying

To garnish:
2 lemon wedges
Parsley sprigs

Imperial

2–3 small fillets lemon sole,
(about 12 oz) skinned
and cut into 1 in strips
2 tablespoons flour
Salt and freshly ground
black pepper
2 eggs, beaten
About 4 oz dried
breadcrumbs
Oil for deep frying

To garnish:
2 lemon wedges
Parsley sprigs

Cooking Time: about 3 minutes

Sole is traditional for these crisp nuggets of fish deep fried in egg and breadcrumbs, but for a more economical starter plaice fillets can be substituted.

Coat the fish in the flour seasoned with salt and pepper, then dip in the egg, making sure that the fish is thoroughly coated. Coat evenly with breadcrumbs, then chill in the refrigerator for approximately 30 minutes.

Pour enough oil for deep-fat frying into a deep-fat fryer and heat gently until the oil is hot enough to turn a stale bread cube golden in 20 to 30 seconds. Put in the fish, increase the heat and fry for approximately 3 minutes or until the goujons are crisp. Drain on absorbent kitchen paper, transfer to a hot serving platter and garnish with lemon wedges and parsley sprigs. Serve immediately with Tartare Sauce handed separately.

Caneton aux cerises

Metric

1 duck (about 2 kg),
with the giblets
25 g butter, softened
Salt and freshly ground
black pepper

For the cherry sauce:
25 g butter
240 g can red cherries,
drained, stoned and
chopped
2 × 15 ml spoons brandy
(optional)
2 × 15 ml spoons redcurrant
jelly
Finely grated rind and
juice of 1 orange
150 ml duck stock (made
with the giblets)
1½ × 5 ml spoons arrowroot
1 × 15 ml spoon water

To garnish:
1 bunch of watercress
Potato crisps

Imperial

1 duck (about 4 lb),
with the giblets
1 oz butter, softened
Salt and freshly ground
black pepper

For the cherry sauce:
1 oz butter
8½ oz can red cherries,
drained, stoned and
chopped
2 tablespoons brandy
(optional)
2 tablespoons redcurrant
jelly
Finely grated rind and
juice of 1 orange
¼ pint duck stock (made
with the giblets)
1½ teaspoons arrowroot
1 tablespoon water

To garnish:
1 bunch of watercress
Potato crisps

Cooking Time: 1½–2 hours
Oven: 200°C, 400°F, Gas Mark 6

It may seem extravagant to serve a whole duck for two persons, but duck is a very bony bird and you will find there is very little left over!

Wash the duck and dry thoroughly with a clean tea-towel or absorbent kitchen paper. Brush the duck with the butter and sprinkle liberally with salt and pepper. Prick all over with a fork and place on a rack in a roasting tin. Roast in a fairly hot oven for 1½–2 hours, turning over occasionally.

Meanwhile, make the cherry sauce: melt the butter in a small pan, add the cherries and heat through. Pour in the brandy, if using, and set alight. Stir in the redcurrant jelly and orange rind and juice, then pour in the stock. Season to taste with salt and pepper. Blend the arrowroot and water together, then stir into the pan. Bring slowly to the boil, stirring constantly, then lower the heat to simmer gently for a few minutes until the sauce thickens. Taste and adjust seasoning.

Transfer the roasted duck to a carving dish and garnish with sprigs of watercress and a few potato crisps. Serve the cherry sauce separately in a sauce boat.

Goujons de sole; Ginger syllabub; Creamed spinach; Caneton aux cerises

Creamed spinach

Metric	Imperial
700 g fresh spinach, washed	*1½ lb fresh spinach, washed*
Salt	*Salt*
25 g butter	*1 oz butter*
3 × 15 ml spoons double cream	*3 tablespoons double cream*
¼ teaspoon grated nutmeg	*¼ teaspoon grated nutmeg*
Freshly ground black pepper	*Freshly ground black pepper*

Cooking Time: 5 to 7 minutes

Put the spinach in a saucepan with the minimum of salted water. Heat gently until the juices flow from the spinach, then cover the pan and cook gently for approximately 5 minutes until the spinach is tender. Drain well and leave to cool in a colander, then purée in an electric blender or work through a Mouli-legumes. Return to the rinsed-out pan, add the butter and heat through. Stir in the cream and nutmeg, then season to taste with salt and pepper. Stir gently until the spinach is hot and combined with the cream and seasonings, then transfer to a warmed serving dish and serve immediately.

Ginger syllabub

Metric	Imperial
2 pieces of whole stem ginger, finely chopped	*2 pieces of whole stem ginger, finely chopped*
2 × 15 ml spoons stem ginger syrup	*2 tablespoons stem ginger syrup*
2 × 15 ml spoons medium or dry sherry	*2 tablespoons medium or dry sherry*
25 g caster sugar	*1 oz caster sugar*
150 ml double cream	*¼ pint double cream*
To finish:	*To finish:*
25 g crystallised ginger, chopped	*1 oz crystallised ginger, chopped*

An old-fashioned English dessert, this Ginger Syllabub is refreshingly light, making a good contrast to a rich main course.

Put the stem ginger and syrup, the sherry and sugar in a bowl and stir to combine. Set aside.

Whip the cream until thick, then fold in the ginger mixture, making sure that it is evenly distributed throughout the cream. Chill in the refrigerator for several hours, then whip again before serving. Spoon into two individual glasses and decorate with the chopped crystallized ginger.

63

Fondue bourguignonne with savoury sauces

Metric	Imperial
1½ kg fillet steak, cut into 2·5 cm cubes	3 lb fillet steak, cut into 1 in cubes
Salt and freshly ground black pepper	Salt and freshly ground black pepper
Vegetable oil for cooking	Vegetable oil for cooking
1 garlic clove, peeled and cut in half (optional)	1 garlic clove, peeled and cut in half (optional)

For the mushroom and tomato sauce:

Metric	Imperial
Vegetable oil for frying	Vegetable oil for frying
1 small onion, peeled and finely chopped	1 small onion, peeled and finely chopped
1 garlic clove, peeled and crushed with ½ teaspoon salt	1 garlic clove, peeled and crushed with ½ teaspoon salt
100 g button mushrooms, cleaned and chopped	4 oz button mushrooms, cleaned and chopped
6 tomatoes, skinned, seeded and chopped	6 tomatoes, skinned, seeded and chopped
Pinch of sugar	Pinch of sugar
Few drops of Tabasco sauce	Few drops of Tabasco sauce
2 × 15 ml spoons tomato chutney	2 tablespoons tomato chutney
150 ml thick mayonnaise (see page 20)	¼ pint thick mayonnaise (see page 20)
Freshly ground black pepper	Freshly ground black pepper

Cooking Time: 8–10 minutes

This is a simple main course to prepare, and guests love to feel they are giving a helping hand with the cooking. Provide them with fondue forks so that they can spear the meat and cook it to their own liking in the oil over the spirit flame. The cooked meat is then dipped into the savoury sauces.

Sprinkle the steak with plenty of salt and pepper and divide into six equal amounts. Arrange on individual plates. Heat the oil slowly in a saucepan on the stove, with the garlic clove (if using). When very hot, pour into a fondue pot and keep hot over a spirit flame on the table. Hand sauces separately; stir before serving.

To make the mushroom and tomato sauce: heat a little oil in a pan, add the onion and garlic and cook gently for approximately 5 minutes until soft and lightly coloured. Add the mushrooms and tomatoes, increase the heat and cook a further few minutes until the mixture thickens and reduces. Remove from the heat, leave to cool, then stir in the remaining ingredients with pepper to taste. Taste and adjust seasoning. Chill in the refrigerator until serving time.

To make the mustard sauce: mix 1 × 5 ml spoon (1 tablespoon) French mustard together with 150 ml (¼ pint) mayonnaise, and a little double cream. Season, stir and chill.

To make the anchovy sauce: drain 1 small can anchovies and pound to a paste, mix with 150 ml (¼ pint) mayonnaise; add capers and seasoning to taste. Chill in the refrigerator until serving time.

Smoked haddock crêpes

Metric	Imperial
300 ml crêpe (pancake) batter (see page 86)	½ pint crêpe (pancake) batter (see page 86)

For the filling:

Metric	Imperial
50 g butter	2 oz butter
50 g flour	2 oz flour
450 ml hot milk	¾ pint hot milk
¼ teaspoon ground mace	¼ teaspoon ground mace
75 g Parmesan cheese, grated	3 oz Parmesan cheese, grated
Freshly ground white pepper	Freshly ground white pepper
350 g smoked haddock, poached in milk, drained, boned and flaked	12 oz smoked haddock, poached in milk, drained, boned and flaked

Cooking Time: 25 minutes

This is an unusual and quite substantial starter. Two crêpes per person is an ample serving.

Make 12 crêpes as in the method on page 86 and keep them warm.

To make the filling: melt the butter in a pan, stir in the flour and cook gently for 1 to 2 minutes, stirring constantly. Remove from the heat and gradually add the hot milk, stirring vigorously. When all the milk is incorporated, return the pan to the heat and bring to the boil, stirring constantly. Lower the heat, add the mace, two-thirds of the Parmesan cheese, and pepper to taste. Simmer gently until the sauce is thick, stirring constantly. Taste and adjust seasoning.

Remove the pan from the heat and pour approximately half the sauce into a mixing bowl. Fold in the flaked fish. Lay the crêpes flat on a board or working surface and put a spoonful of filling on each one. Roll up the crêpes and place in a single layer in a shallow heatproof serving dish. Pour over the remaining sauce, sprinkle with the remaining Parmesan cheese and put under a preheated hot grill for a few minutes until the top is golden brown. Serve hot straight from the dish.

French potato casserole

French potato casserole

Metric	Imperial
About 1½ kg potatoes, peeled	About 3 lb potatoes, peeled
Salt	Salt
50 g butter, softened	2 oz butter, softened
Freshly ground black pepper	Freshly ground black pepper
6 × 15 ml spoons milk	6 tablespoons milk
6 × 15 ml spoons single cream	6 tablespoons single cream
50 g Gruyère or Emmenthal cheese, grated	2 oz Gruyère or Emmenthal cheese, grated

Cooking Time: 1 hour
Oven: 190°C, 375°F, Gas Mark 5

This casserole makes a substantial vegetable dish to serve with Fondue Bourguignonne, and no other vegetable should be needed apart from a green salad
Blanch the potatoes in boiling salted water for 5 minutes, then drain and leave until cool enough to handle. Slice the potatoes thickly.
Brush the inside of a large casserole dish with some of the butter. Arrange a layer of potato slices in the bottom, sprinkle with salt and pepper and dot with some more of the butter. Pour in 1 × 15 ml spoon (1 tablespoon) each of milk and cream. Continue with these layers until all the ingredients are used up, pouring in any remaining milk and cream at the end. Sprinkle the top of casserole with the grated cheese and more salt and pepper.
Bake, uncovered, in a fairly hot oven for about 1 hour until the top is golden brown and the potatoes are tender when pierced. Serve hot straight from the casserole.

Crème brûlée with sugared raspberries

Crème brûlée with sugared raspberries

Metric	Imperial
100 g caster sugar	4 oz caster sugar
2 × 5 ml spoons vanilla essence	2 teaspoons vanilla essence
6 egg yolks	6 egg yolks
900 ml double cream	1½ pints double cream
50 g demerara sugar	2 oz demerara sugar
350 g fresh or frozen raspberries, thawed	12 oz fresh or frozen raspberries, thawed

Cooking Time: 1¼ hours
Oven: 150°C, 300°F, Gas Mark 2

Any soft summer fruit can be substituted for the raspberries that top this dessert.

Put two-thirds of the caster sugar, the vanilla essence and egg yolks in a bowl and beat to combine without allowing to become frothy. Set aside.

Put the cream in the top of a double boiler or in a heatproof bowl standing on top of a pan of gently simmering water. Heat until just below boiling point, then immediately pour into the egg yolk mixture, stirring to combine. Strain into a baking dish and put in a bain marie or roasting pan half filled with hot water.

Bake in a cool oven for 1¼ hours or until just set. Remove dish from bain marie, leave until cold, then chill in the refrigerator, overnight if possible. When chilled, sprinkle with the demerara sugar and put under a preheated hot grill until the sugar caramelises.

Remove from grill and leave to cool again. Meanwhile, toss the raspberries in the remaining caster sugar. Cover the top of the crème brulée with the sugared raspberries and serve chilled straight from the baking dish.

Easter is second only to Christmas in being one of the most celebrated of Christian festivals, yet many of our Easter customs are pagan in origin. Hot Cross Buns are believed to have been eaten before Christian times when the cross was made to depict the sun and the fire. Nowadays, Hot Cross Buns and Easter Biscuits are traditionally eaten on Good Friday, the cross on the buns being of religious significance; and roast spring lamb is served for lunch on Easter Sunday to represent the innocence of Christ.

Hot cross squares

Metric

*25 g fresh yeast, or 4 ×
5 ml spoons dried yeast
and 1 × 5 ml spoon sugar
300 ml warm milk and
water mixed
450 g strong plain flour
1 × 5 ml spoon salt
½ teaspoon mixed spice
½ teaspoon ground
cinnamon
½ teaspoon grated nutmeg
50 g caster sugar
50 g butter
1 egg, beaten
50 g currants
50 g chopped mixed peel*

To finish:
*100 g shortcrust pastry
dough (made with 100 g
flour, 50 g butter, 1
× 15 ml spoon water)
50 g sugar
2 × 15 ml spoons water*

Imperial

*1 oz fresh yeast, or 4
teaspoons dried yeast
and 1 teaspoon sugar
½ pint warm milk and
water mixed
1 lb strong plain flour
1 teaspoon salt
½ teaspoon mixed spice
½ teaspoon ground
cinnamon
½ teaspoon grated nutmeg
2 oz caster sugar
2 oz butter
1 egg, beaten
2 oz currants
2 oz chopped mixed peel*

To finish:
*4 oz shortcrust pastry
dough (made with 4 oz
flour, 2 oz butter, 1
tablespoon water)
2 oz sugar
2 tablespoons water*

Cooking Time: 20 minutes
Oven: 190°C, 375°F, Gas Mark 5

This is a simple variation of the traditional hot cross buns. If you prefer, you can still form the dough into bun shapes and bake on greased baking sheets.

Cream the fresh yeast with a little of the milk and water. (If using dried yeast, stir the sugar into the milk and water and sprinkle the dried yeast over.) Leave in a warm place for 10 minutes or until frothy.

Meanwhile sieve the flour, salt and spices into a warm mixing bowl. Stir in the caster sugar. Rub in the butter with the fingertips. Make a well in the centre of the flour, pour in the frothy yeast mixture and liquid, the egg, currants and mixed peel. Mix together with the hands until a soft dough is formed. Turn out on to a lightly floured board and knead for 10 minutes until smooth. Roll out the dough to a rectangle to fit a roasting pan about 30 cm (12 in) × 23 cm (9 in), brush the inside of the pan with butter and put in the dough. Mark into twelve squares with a sharp knife. Leave in a warm place for approximately 1 hour until almost doubled in bulk.

Roll out the shortcrust pastry dough on a floured board and cut into three 30 cm (12 in) strips and four 23 cm (9 in) strips. Place the strips on top of the risen dough, forming a criss-cross pattern to make crosses on the twelve squares. Use a little water to stick the strips on.

Bake in the centre of a fairly hot oven for 20 minutes or until browned on top. Remove from the oven, leave to cool for a few minutes, then cut into twelve squares. Transfer squares to a wire rack.

Put the sugar and water into a heavy-based pan and heat gently until the sugar has dissolved. Increase the heat and boil rapidly for a few minutes until a syrup is formed. Remove from the heat and brush over the squares until all the syrup is used. Leave until cool before splitting in two and spreading with butter.

To freeze: open freeze until solid, then pack in a single layer in rigid containers or freezer bags. Seal, label and return to freezer.

To thaw: leave in wrappings for about 45 minutes at room temperature, then unwrap, place on a baking sheet and refresh in a fairly hot oven for 5 to 10 minutes until warmed through.

Makes 12

Hot cross squares

Carrot and tomato soup

Metric

25 g butter
1 large onion, peeled and
finely chopped
450 g carrots, scraped
and chopped
396 g can tomatoes
1 × 5 ml spoon sugar
600 ml chicken stock
Finely grated rind and
juice of 1 orange
Salt and freshly ground
black pepper

To garnish:
3 × 15 ml spoons finely
chopped parsley

Imperial

1 oz butter
1 large onion, peeled and
finely chopped
1 lb carrots, scraped
and chopped
14 oz can tomatoes
1 teaspoon sugar
1 pint chicken stock
Finely grated rind and
juice of 1 orange
Salt and freshly ground
black pepper

To garnish:
3 tablespoons finely
chopped parsley

Cooking Time: 25 to 30 minutes

Sweet, early carrots give this soup its refreshing flavour and light texture.

Melt the butter in a heavy saucepan, add the onion and cook gently for approximately 5 minutes until soft and lightly coloured. Stir in the carrots, cover the vegetables with greaseproof paper, then cover the pan and cook over a very low heat for another 5 minutes.

Remove the lid and greaseproof paper, stir in the tomatoes, sugar, stock, orange rind and juice and season to taste with salt and pepper. Bring to the boil, stirring, then lower the heat, half cover with the lid and simmer for 10 to 15 minutes until the carrots are tender. Remove from the heat and leave to cool a little. Purée in an electric blender or work through a Mouli-legumes until smooth. Return the soup to the rinsed-out pan and heat through. If the soup is too thick, stir in a little chicken stock, milk or water. Taste and adjust seasoning. Pour into warmed soup bowls and sprinkle each with a little parsley. Serve immediately.

To freeze: pour cooled soup into a rigid container, leaving head space. Seal, label and freeze.

To thaw: reheat soup from frozen in a saucepan over gentle heat, stirring constantly. Garnish with parsley just before serving.

Serves 4–6

Tarte au citron; Carrot and tomato soup; Spiced leg of lamb

Spiced leg of lamb

Metric	Imperial
1 × 2 kg leg of lamb	1 × 4 lb leg of lamb
1 garlic clove, peeled and cut into slivers	1 garlic clove, peeled and cut into slivers
1 × 15 ml spoon ground coriander	1 tablespoon ground coriander
1 × 15 ml spoon ground cumin	1 tablespoon ground cumin
1 × 15 ml spoon flour	1 tablespoon flour
6 black peppercorns, crushed	6 black peppercorns, crushed
1 × 5 ml spoon salt	1 teaspoon salt
2 × 15 ml spoons tomato purée	2 tablespoons tomato purée
2 × 5 ml spoons lemon juice	2 teaspoons lemon juice
50 g lard or dripping	2 oz lard or dripping
450 ml hot beef stock	¾ pint hot beef stock

Cooking Time: 1¾ hours
Oven: 230°C, 450°F, Gas Mark 8;
        180°C, 350°F, Gas Mark 4

Serve this joint of lamb with a medley of fresh spring vegetables—imported new potatoes, peas and carrots are just coming into the shops around Easter time.

Score the skin of the lamb and insert the garlic slivers. Mix together the spices, flour, peppercorns, salt, tomato purée and lemon juice in a bowl and brush all over the lamb. Chill in the refrigerator overnight. Put the lamb in a roasting pan with the lard or dripping. Roast on the top shelf of a very hot oven for 15 to 20 minutes until the meat is browned, basting occasionally. Pour the hot stock into the pan, lower the heat to moderate and roast for approximately 1½ hours or until the juices run pink when the meat is pierced with a skewer. Spoon the stock over the lamb from time to time during cooking.

Remove the meat from the pan and leave in a warm place before carving. Transfer the pan to the top of the stove and boil the stock to reduce to a thick gravy. Taste and adjust seasoning before serving.

Serves 4–6

Tarte au citron

Metric	Imperial
175 g sweet shortcrust pastry (see page 80)	6 oz sweet shortcrust pastry (see page 80)
For the filling:	**For the filling:**
50 g butter	2 oz butter
Finely grated rind and juice of 2 lemons	Finely grated rind and juice of 2 lemons
2 eggs, beaten	2 eggs, beaten
225 g caster sugar	8 oz caster sugar
75 g ground almonds	3 oz ground almonds
For the topping:	**For the topping:**
2 lemons, thinly sliced, pips removed	2 lemons, thinly sliced, pips removed
For the glaze:	**For the glaze:**
Water	Water
225 g sugar	8 oz sugar

Cooking Time: 20–25 minutes
Oven: 190°C, 375°F, Gas Mark 5

Roll out the shortcrust pastry and line a 20 cm (8 in) flan dish or flan ring placed on a baking sheet. Flute the edges and prick the base, then chill the dough in the refrigerator for another 30 minutes. Line the dough with foil and baking beans and bake blind in a fairly hot oven for 10 minutes. Remove foil and beans, return to the oven and bake for another 10 to 15 minutes until the pastry is golden and set. Remove and leave to cool.

Put the ingredients for the filling (except the ground almonds) in the top of a double boiler or in a heatproof bowl standing over a pan of gently simmering water. Cook the mixture for 30 to 40 minutes until thick, stirring constantly with a wooden spoon. Remove from the heat and stir in the ground almonds until evenly mixed. Pour into the flan case and leave to set in a cool place overnight. Meanwhile, prepare the lemon slices for the top of the tart. Put the slices in a heatproof bowl, pour over boiling water to cover and leave overnight. The next day, drain the slices, put in a pan and cover with fresh water. Bring to the boil and simmer gently for 20 to 30 minutes until they are soft. Remove lemon slices with a slotted spoon, reserving the cooking liquid. Dry on absorbent kitchen paper, then arrange on top of the set filling.

To prepare the glaze: make the reserved cooking liquid from the lemon slices up to 300 ml/½ pint with water. Put in a heavy-based pan with the sugar and heat gently until the sugar has dissolved. Increase the heat and boil rapidly for 7 to 10 minutes until syrupy. Remove from the heat, leave to cool slightly, then spoon over the lemon slices to cover. Leave to set, then remove flan ring, if used. Place flan on a serving platter before serving.

Serves 4–6

Coloured eggs

Coloured eggs

These are traditional at Easter–particularly in Eastern Europe–and are very simple to make. If you wish to paint decorations or elaborate designs on eggs, then you must hard-boil them for 12 minutes before working on them. Eggs can be left white or coloured by steeping in fabric dyes after hard-boiling. Use fine-nibbed felt tip pens for decorating eggs, etching in the design with a faint pencil beforehand. Allow each side of the egg to dry before working round the egg. Hard-boiled eggs will keep indefinitely if the shells are kept intact, and they make a most attractive Easter decoration.

To colour eggs with food colouring: put 2×5 ml spoons (2 teaspoons) food colouring–red, cochineal, blue, yellow etc.–into a saucepan of boiling water and stir well. Put in the quantity of white-shelled eggs you wish to colour and boil for 10 minutes or until the egg shells become coloured. The eggs will take on delicate, pale colours which can be improved by rubbing gently with a little oil after the eggs have cooled.

To colour eggs yellow or rust with onion skins: put the skins of several onions in a pan with plenty of cold water (add 2×5 ml spoons (2 teaspoons) malt vinegar for a rust colour). Bring to the boil, then simmer gently until the water becomes coloured. The longer the skins are simmered, the deeper the colour. Strain into a bowl. Put hard-boiled white eggs into the strained liquid and leave to steep until the desired colour is obtained. Remove from the liquid with a slotted spoon, pat dry with absorbent kitchen paper, then brush lightly with oil and buff with more paper or a duster. Leave plain or decorate as above and keep indefinitely.

Paskha

Paskha

Metric	Imperial
50 g maraschino cherries, drained and chopped	*2 oz maraschino cherries, drained and chopped*
50 g chopped mixed peel	*2 oz chopped mixed peel*
50 g blanched almonds, finely chopped	*2 oz blanched almonds, finely chopped*
50 g seedless raisins	*2 oz seedless raisins*
Finely grated rind of 1 lemon	*Finely grated rind of 1 lemon*
1 × 15 ml spoon dry sherry	*1 tablespoon dry sherry*
350 g carton cottage cheese	*12 oz carton cottage cheese*
100 g cream cheese	*4 oz cream cheese*
100 g caster sugar	*4 oz caster sugar*
120 ml carton double cream	*4 fl oz carton double cream*
2 × 5 ml spoons powdered gelatine	*2 teaspoons powdered gelatine*
3 × 15 ml spoons lemon juice	*3 tablespoons lemon juice*

To garnish:
A little oil
About 12 glacé cherries, halved

To garnish:
A little oil
About 12 glacé cherries, halved

Paskha is a Russian Easter speciality, a kind of uncooked cheesecake mixed with fruit and nuts. This is a simplified English version and is delicious served for a dessert, or at teatime.

Put the maraschino cherries, mixed peel, almonds, raisins and lemon rind in a small bowl, stir in the sherry and mix well until the sherry is absorbed. Set aside.

Mix the cottage and cream cheeses together, then beat in the sugar. Beat the cream until thick and fold into the cheese with the fruit and nut mixture.

Sprinkle the gelatine over the lemon juice in a small heatproof bowl, leave until spongy, then place the bowl in a pan of hot water and stir over low heat until the gelatine has dissolved. Remove from the heat, leave to cool slightly, then fold into the cheese mixture. Line a 12.5 cm (5 in) clay flower pot with a large piece of muslin or a clean tea-towel, spoon in the cheese and fold the cloth over the top. Cover with a saucer, place heavy weights on top, stand in a bowl and chill in the refrigerator overnight.

The next day, remove the weights and saucer and unfold the cloth. Invert a serving platter over the pot and turn out the paskha. Brush lightly with oil, then press halved glacé cherries around the top and bottom edges. Chill in the refrigerator until serving time.

Serves 6–8

73

French Easter cake

Metric

For the Genoese sponge:
75 g flour, sieved
25 g cornflour, sieved
4 eggs, beaten
100 g caster sugar
100 g unsalted butter,
melted and cooled

For the butter icing:
175 g butter
450 g icing sugar, sieved
2 × 15 ml spoons hot
water
100 g plain cooking
chocolate, broken into
pieces
2 × 15 ml spoons liquid
coffee

To finish:
Few miniature Easter eggs

Imperial

For the Genoese sponge:
3 oz flour, sieved
1 oz cornflour, sieved
4 eggs beaten
4 oz caster sugar
4 oz unsalted butter,
melted and cooled

For the butter icing:
6 oz butter
1 lb icing sugar, sieved
2 tablespoons hot
water
4 oz plain cooking
chocolate, broken into
pieces
2 tablespoons liquid
coffee

To finish:
Few miniature Easter eggs

Cooking Time: 20–25 minutes
Oven: 190°C, 375°F, Gas Mark 5

To make the sponge: grease three 18 cm (7 in) round shallow cake tins and line the bases.
Sieve the flour and cornflour together and set aside. Put the eggs and sugar in a heatproof bowl and stand over a pan of simmering water. Beat with a balloon whisk, electric or rotary beater until the mixture becomes thick. Remove from the heat and continue beating until the mixture is cool. Slowly stir the melted butter into the mixture from the side of the bowl, then sieve half the flour and cornflour over the bowl and fold in gently. Repeat with the remaining flour and cornflour.
Pour the mixture into the prepared tins and bake in the centre of a fairly hot oven for 20 to 25 minutes, until well risen and firm to the touch.
Meanwhile, make the butter cream: beat the butter in a bowl until light, then gradually beat in the icing sugar a little at a time, adding hot water as the mixture becomes too stiff to beat. Put one quarter of the butter cream in a separate bowl. Set aside. Put the chocolate pieces and liquid coffee in a heatproof bowl and stand over a pan of gently simmering water. Heat gently until the chocolate has melted, stirring occasionally, then remove from the heat and stir into the separate quarter of butter cream. Spread some of this chocolate butter cream on top of two of the cakes and sandwich the three cakes together. Put the cake on a stand and spread the top and sides with most of the unflavoured butter cream.
Stir the leftover unflavoured butter cream into the remaining chocolate butter cream and put into a forcing bag fitted with a small star tube. Pipe small stars around the top edge of the cake and join the stars together by piping a line between each one. Pipe vertical lines around the sides of the cake beneath the stars, working from the bottom upwards. Repeat the top edge decoration around the bottom of the cake and decorate with Easter eggs.
Cuts into 8–10 slices

Easter biscuits

Metric

75 g butter or margarine
75 g caster sugar
1 egg, beaten
175 g self-raising flour
Pinch of salt
½ teaspoon mixed spice
50 g currants
1–2 × 15 ml spoons milk

To finish:
1 egg white, lightly beaten
Caster sugar for sprinkling

Imperial

3 oz butter or margarine
3 oz caster sugar
1 egg, beaten
6 oz self-raising flour
Pinch of salt
½ teaspoon mixed spice
2 oz currants
1–2 tablespoons milk

To finish:
1 egg white, lightly beaten
Caster sugar for sprinkling

Cooking Time: 20 minutes
Oven: 180°C, 350°F, Gas Mark 4

Cream together the butter or margarine and sugar in a mixing bowl until light and fluffy, then beat in the egg. Sieve the flour, salt and mixed spice and fold into the creamed mixture with the currants. Beat well to mix, adding enough milk to make a soft pliable dough. Knead lightly until the dough is smooth, then roll out on a floured board to 6 mm (¼ in) thick. Stamp into rounds. Put biscuits on greased baking sheets, allowing room for expansion. Bake in the centre of a moderate oven for 10 minutes. Remove from the oven, brush with the egg white and sprinkle with caster sugar. Return to the oven and continue cooking for a further 10 minutes or until the biscuits are golden and crisp. When cooked, leave biscuits to cool for a few minutes. Transfer to a wire rack to cool completely. Store in an airtight tin.
Makes 16–18

French Easter cake; Easter biscuits

Everyone looks forward to the traditional fare of Christmastide and the Christmas dinner should be a meal to remember. Ever since Elizabethan days, roast goose has been the traditional bird for the Christmas table, although in recent years turkey has become more popular – at least in this country. The recipe for Roast Goose with two stuffings in this chapter will be ample for six, but if you have a larger gathering it would perhaps be wiser to serve turkey – a far meatier bird than goose and one that will provide you with many more meals for the days after Christmas. If you are entertaining at Christmas you will obviously have to plan all the meals down to the last detail. Both the Plum Pudding and the Christmas Cake can be made long before the festive season – plum pudding will keep for as long as 12 months, or more if stored in a cool, dry place; so too will the cake without its almond paste and royal icing.

Roast goose with stuffings

Metric

1 × 4 kg goose, trussed and cleaned, with giblets
2 × 15 ml spoons clear honey
Salt and freshly ground black pepper

For the sausagemeat and apple stuffing:
50 g butter
2 medium-sized onions, peeled and finely chopped
Liver from goose, finely chopped
225 g pork sausagemeat
2 large cooking apples
175 g brown breadcrumbs

For the sage and onion stuffing:
50 g butter
450 g onions, peeled and finely chopped
350 g fresh white breadcrumbs
1 egg, beaten
3 × 15 ml spoons dried sage
3–4 × 15 ml spoons single cream or top of the milk

Imperial

1 × 9 lb goose, trussed and cleaned, with giblets
2 tablespoons clear honey
Salt and freshly ground black pepper

For the sausagemeat and apple stuffing:
2 oz butter
2 medium-sized onions, peeled and finely chopped
Liver from goose, finely chopped
8 oz pork sausagemeat
2 large cooking apples
6 oz brown breadcrumbs

For the sage and onion stuffing:
2 oz butter
1 lb onions, peeled and finely chopped
12 oz fresh white breadcrumbs
1 egg, beaten
3 tablespoons dried sage
3–4 tablespoons single cream or top of the milk

Cooking Time: 3–3½ hours
Oven: 200°C, 400°F, Gas Mark 6;
180°C, 350°F, Gas Mark 4

The traditional stuffing for Christmas Roast Goose is sage and onion, but sausagemeat and apple makes an unusual alternative. Choose one or the other, or stuff the goose with sausagemeat and apple, then form the sage and onion into small balls, coat in flour and shallow fry until crisp. Arrange around the goose when serving. To make the sausagemeat and apple stuffing: melt the butter in a pan, add the onions and cook gently until golden. Add the liver and sausagemeat and cook until browned, breaking up and stirring constantly. Peel, core and chop the apples and add to the pan. Continue cooking for 5 minutes, stirring constantly, then transfer to a bowl and stir in the breadcrumbs. Season and mix well.

To make the sage and onion stuffing: melt the butter in a pan, add the onions and cook gently until golden. Transfer to a bowl and stir in the breadcrumbs, egg and sage. Mix well, adding enough cream or milk to hold the stuffing together. Season to taste with salt and pepper. Spoon the chosen stuffing into the cavity of the goose, then sew up both openings with trussing string. Secure with skewers if necessary. Place the goose on a rack in a roasting pan, brush with the honey and sprinkle liberally with salt and pepper. Roast in a fairly hot oven for 30 minutes to brown the skin, then cover the bird with foil, reduce the heat to moderate and roast for another 2½ to 3 hours or until the juices run clear when the goose is pierced with a skewer. Baste and turn the bird frequently during cooking, and pour off excess fat. Remove the bird from the oven and discard strings and skewers, if used. Transfer to a warmed serving platter and serve with roast potatoes, seasonal vegetables and a well-flavoured giblet gravy made with the pan juices.
Serves 6

Roast goose with stuffings

Bread sauce ; Cranberry sauce

Cranberry sauce

Metric	Imperial
225 g fresh or frozen cranberries	8 oz fresh or frozen cranberries
100–150 g sugar	4–6 oz sugar
Finely grated rind and juice of 1 orange	Finely grated rind and juice of 1 orange

Cooking Time: 30 minutes

The sharp flavour of cranberries with a hint of sweet orange makes a welcome contrast to the richness of other Christmas fare.

Put the cranberries in a pan, stir in 100 g (4 oz) of sugar and the orange rind and juice. Pour in enough water to just cover the fruit and bring to the boil. Lower the heat and simmer the sauce gently for about 30 minutes until the cranberries are tender and split open.

Remove sauce from the heat, leave to cool slightly, then rub through a sieve. Taste and add more sugar if necessary. Pour into a serving bowl and chill in the refrigerator until serving time.

To freeze: cover bowl with cling film and pack in a freezer bag. Or transfer sauce to a rigid container. Seal, label and freeze.

To thaw: leave in wrappings at room temperature for 3–4 hours.

Serves 6

Bread sauce

Metric	Imperial
1 onion, peeled and stuck with 6 cloves	1 onion, peeled and stuck with 6 cloves
450 ml milk	$\frac{3}{4}$ pint milk
$\frac{1}{4}$ teaspoon ground mace	$\frac{1}{4}$ teaspoon ground mace
6 black peppercorns, crushed	6 black peppercorns, crushed
1 bay leaf, crushed	1 bay leaf, crushed
$\frac{1}{2}$ teaspoon salt	$\frac{1}{2}$ teaspoon salt
100 g fresh white breadcrumbs	4 oz fresh white breadcrumbs
25 g butter	1 oz butter

Cooking Time: 5–7 minutes

A flavoursome bread sauce is an essential part of the traditional festive table. Serve it with roast chicken, turkey or pheasant.

Put the onion in a pan, pour in the milk, then add the mace, peppercorns, bay leaf and salt. Bring slowly to the boil, then turn off the heat, cover the pan with a lid and leave to infuse for 15 to 20 minutes. Strain the milk, then return to the rinsed-out pan, add the breadcrumbs and butter and simmer gently until hot and thickened, stirring occasionally. Taste and adjust seasoning before serving.

Serves 6

Rum butter; Brandy butter

Brandy and rum butters

Metric	Imperial
100 g unsalted butter, softened	4 oz unsalted butter, softened
100 g icing sugar, sieved	4 oz icing sugar, sieved
Finely grated rind and juice of 1 lemon	Finely grated rind and juice of 1 lemon
3–4 × 15 ml spoons brandy	3–4 tablespoons brandy

Rich plum pudding topped with lashings of brandy or rum butter is traditional at Christmas time, and home-made butters are far superior to any of the commercial varieties available.

Put the butter in a mixing bowl and beat until light and fluffy. Gradually add the icing sugar a little at a time, beating vigorously until all is incorporated. Beat in the lemon rind and juice, and brandy to taste. Spoon into a serving bowl and chill in the refrigerator until needed.

To freeze: cover bowl with cling film or foil and pack in a freezer bag. Or transfer butter to a rigid container. Seal, label and freeze.

To thaw: leave in wrappings in the refrigerator overnight. Makes enough for 6 servings.

Variation

Rum butter

Make as for Brandy Butter above, substituting orange rind and juice and rum for the lemon and brandy.

Mincemeat

Metric	Imperial
450 ml medium or dry cider	¾ pint medium or dry cider
450 g dark soft brown sugar	1 lb dark soft brown sugar
2 kg cooking apples	4 lb cooking apples
1 × 5 ml spoon mixed spice	1 teaspoon mixed spice
1 × 5 ml spoon ground cinnamon	1 teaspoon ground cinnamon
450 g currants	1 lb currants
450 g seedless raisins	1 lb seedless raisins
100 g glacé cherries, finely chopped	4 oz glacé cherries, finely chopped
100 g blanched almonds, finely chopped	4 oz blanched almonds, finely chopped
Finely grated rind and juice of 1 lemon	Finely grated rind and juice of 1 lemon
1 miniature bottle brandy or rum	1 miniature bottle brandy or rum

Cooking Time: 30–40 minutes

This is an unusual mincemeat recipe using a fairly high proportion of cooking apples, and no suet. The mincemeat itself is boiled before packing into jars and storing – this makes it keep well. Make it in the autumn when cooking apples are plentiful, then store it in a cool dry place until Christmas.

Put the cider and sugar in a large saucepan and heat gently until the sugar has dissolved.

Meanwhile, peel, core and chop the apples and add to the pan. Stir in the remaining ingredients, except the brandy or rum, and bring slowly to the boil, stirring constantly. Lower the heat, half cover with a lid and simmer for approximately 30 minutes or until the mincemeat has become a soft pulp, stirring occasionally. Turn off the heat and leave mincemeat until quite cold. Stir in the brandy or rum, making sure that it is evenly distributed. Spoon the mincemeat into clean, dry jars with screw-topped lids, covering the top of mincemeat with a circle of greaseproof paper before putting on lids.

Makes about 4 kg (8 lb)

Mincemeat flan

Metric	Imperial
For the pastry:	**For the pastry:**
250 g flour	8 oz flour
Pinch of salt	Pinch of salt
125 g butter or margarine	4 oz butter or margarine
2 × 15 ml spoons caster sugar	2 tablespoons caster sugar
1 egg yolk	1 egg yolk
2 × 15 ml spoons cold water	2 tablespoons cold water
For the filling:	**For the filling:**
6 dessert apples	6 dessert apples
50 g butter	2 oz butter
75 g demerara sugar	3 oz demerara sugar
Finely grated rind and juice of 1 lemon	Finely grated rind and juice of 1 lemon
300 g mincemeat	10 oz mincemeat
For the topping:	**For the topping:**
3 egg whites	3 egg whites
175 g caster sugar	6 oz caster sugar

Cooking Time: 50 minutes
Oven: 190°C, 375°F, Gas Mark 5;
     140°C, 275°F, Gas Mark 1

To save time during the Christmas holiday, you may freeze this flan before adding the meringue topping. To serve, thaw the flan, coat in the meringue and bake.

Sieve the flour and salt into a bowl. Add the butter or margarine in pieces and rub into the flour until the mixture resembles fine breadcrumbs. Stir in the caster sugar and egg yolk, then stir in the water and draw the dough together to form a smooth ball. Wrap in foil and chill in the refrigerator for 30 minutes. Roll out the dough on a lightly floured board to a circle large enough to line a 23 cm (9 in) flan tin or flan ring placed on a baking sheet. Prick the base of the dough with a fork and chill in the refrigerator for another 30 minutes. Line the dough with foil and baking beans and bake blind in a fairly hot oven for 15 minutes. Remove foil and beans, return to the oven and bake for another 5 minutes until the pastry is golden. Remove the flan ring if used.

Peel apples, core with an apple corer and slice into thin rings. Melt the butter in a pan, add the apple rings, demerara sugar, lemon rind and juice and cook gently for a few minutes until the apples are coated in the mixture. Cool. Arrange half the apple rings in the bottom of the pastry case, spoon in the mincemeat and top with the remaining apples.

Beat the egg whites until stiff, then beat in 1 × 15 ml spoon (1 tablespoon) of the caster sugar. Fold in the remaining sugar, reserving 1 × 15 ml spoon (1 tablespoon) for dredging. Pipe the meringue on top of the flan to cover the filling completely. Dredge with the reserved sugar and bake in a very cool oven for 30 minutes until the meringue is golden. Remove from the oven and leave to rest for approximately 15 minutes before serving.

Cuts into 12 wedges

Mincemeat flan; Mincemeat; Plum pudding

Plum pudding

Metric

*225 g pitted prunes, soaked
overnight in cold water,
drained and finely chopped*
225 g seedless raisins
225 g sultanas
225 g currants
225 g mixed dried fruit
*225 g carrots, peeled
and grated*
225 g shredded beef suet
*450 g fresh white
breadcrumbs*
225 g self-raising flour
225 g sugar
¼ teaspoon salt
½ teaspoon baking powder
½ teaspoon mixed spice
½ teaspoon grated nutmeg
*Finely grated rind and
juice of 1 lemon*
3 eggs, beaten
300 ml stout
Milk to mix
Flour for sealing

Imperial

*8 oz pitted prunes, soaked
overnight in cold water,
drained and finely chopped*
8 oz seedless raisins
8 oz sultanas
8 oz currants
8 oz mixed dried fruit
*8 oz carrots, peeled and
grated*
8 oz shredded beef suet
*1 lb fresh white
breadcrumbs*
8 oz self-raising flour
8 oz sugar
¼ teaspoon salt
½ teaspoon baking powder
½ teaspoon mixed spice
½ teaspoon grated nutmeg
*Finely grated rind and
juice of 1 lemon*
3 eggs, beaten
½ pint stout
Milk to mix
Flour for sealing

Cooking Time: 6 hours

This is a very old recipe for a traditional, rich Christmas pudding, and it is one that improves in flavour the longer it is kept. If you like, you can continue the old custom of burying a silver threepenny or sixpenny piece in the pudding before steaming–but wrap it in foil first.

Put the dried fruit, carrots, suet, breadcrumbs, self-raising flour and sugar in a large mixing bowl and stir well to mix. Add the remaining dry ingredients and stir to combine. Stir in the lemon rind and juice, eggs and stout and continue stirring until all the ingredients are thoroughly combined, adding enough milk to make a soft dropping consistency.

Spoon the mixture into greased pudding basins to come within 2·5 cm (1 in) of each rim, packing the mixture down well with the back of a spoon. Cover the top of each with a circle of greased greaseproof paper. Put a thick layer of flour on top of the greaseproof, pressing it down well with the back of a spoon, then cover with another circle of greaseproof paper. Cover the basins with a pudding cloth, muslin or aluminium foil, leaving room for the puddings to rise during cooking. Tie securely.

Place the puddings in the top of a steamer or double boiler, or in a large pan of gently bubbling water, and steam for at least six hours, topping up the water level from time to time during cooking.

Remove puddings from the pan and leave until cold. Check that the puddings are tightly sealed–the flour will have become a solid paste–and renew the top piece of greaseproof and the cloth if necessary. Store in a cool dry place. Steam again for 2 to 3 hours before serving.

Makes about 5 × 450 g (1 lb) puddings.

81

Rum truffles

Metric

100 g plain chocolate, broken into pieces
3 × 15 ml spoons rum
100 g stale fruit cake
100 g ground almonds
50 g icing sugar, sifted
2 × 15 ml spoons apricot jam, sieved
15 g cocoa powder
50 g chocolate vermicelli

Imperial

4 oz plain chocolate, broken into pieces
3 tablespoons rum
4 oz stale fruit cake
4 oz ground almonds
2 oz icing sugar, sifted
2 tablespoons apricot jam, sieved
½ oz cocoa powder
2 oz chocolate vermicelli

Truffles make pretty presents if packaged in a festive-looking box, or they can be handed round with the coffee and liqueurs after Christmas dinner.

Put the chocolate and rum in a heatproof bowl and stand over a pan of gently simmering water. Heat until the chocolate melts, stirring occasionally.

Meanwhile, crumble the cake and ground almonds together in a bowl with the fingertips. Pour in the melted chocolate and the icing sugar and stir well to combine. Turn out on to a board sprinkled with icing sugar and knead lightly until smooth.

Shape the mixture into approximately 25 balls and brush with the jam. Put the cocoa and vermicelli together in a bowl and shake to combine. Add the truffles one at a time and shake the bowl until each truffle is evenly coated. Chill in the refrigerator until firm, then pack in sweet cases.

To freeze: open freeze until solid, then pack carefully in a single layer in a rigid container. Seal, label and return to freezer.

To thaw: put frozen truffles in sweet cases and thaw for approximately 1 hour at room temperature.
Makes about 25

Rum truffles

Christmas cake

The basic design for this cake is simple, yet effective. Make the cake in three easy stages, starting it during the month of November, then there will be very little to do during the days immediately before Christmas. Follow the instructions for the Anniversary Cake (page 26), baking the rich fruit mixture in a 25 cm (10 in) round cake tin. Leave to mature for one month, spooning over more spirits from time to time, if wished. Coat with the same quantity of almond paste as the Anniversary Cake, then leave to dry out for one week.

To decorate the cake:

1. Make up the same quantity of royal icing as for the Anniversary Cake (without food colouring) and use to coat the cake. Quickly scoop up the surplus icing, put in a bowl and cover with a lid or damp cloth. Leave cake and surplus icing overnight.
2. The next day, lift the cake on to a 30 cm (12 in) round silver cake board. Thicken the surplus icing with the remaining icing sugar as for the Anniversary Cake. Fit a piping bag with a No. 8 star tube, put in some of the icing and pipe a large shell edge around the base of the cake to neaten it and join it to the board.
3. Fit a piping bag with a No. 2 plain tube, put in some of the icing and pipe a diagonal line across the cake 1·5 cm (½ in) in from the centre. Pipe five lines parallel to this line 6 mm (¼ in) apart. Repeat these five lines at right angles on the other side of the cake, then overpipe each line on both sides. Neaten the ends of the lines by piping a small beading.
4. Using the No. 2 plain tube, pipe the words 'Merry Christmas' in the large triangle formed by the lines. In the three remaining triangles pipe outlines of holly leaves and small circles for berries.
5. Put 3 × 15 ml spoons (3 tablespoons) of the remaining icing in a separate bowl and thin it down with a little water to a running consistency. Colour it with a few drops of green food colouring. Make a plain greaseproof paper cone, put in the green icing and cut the end of the cone. Use to fill in the holly shapes.
6. Colour the remaining icing with a few drops of bright red food colouring and put into a piping bag fitted with a No. 2 plain tube. Overpipe the lines on the top of the cake and the lettering. Fill in the circles to represent holly berries. Pipe a looped line over the shell edging at the base of the cake.
7. Leave the icing to dry, then tie a red ribbon or cake frill around the cake.

Christmas cake

January 25th, the birthday of the Scottish poet Robert Burns, is Burns' Night – one of the nights in the year when it is customary to eat haggis. A traditional haggis contains the minced lights, liver and heart of a sheep, together with beef suet, onions, oatmeal, gravy and plenty of seasoning. This mixture is put into a sheep's stomach or paunch and boiled for several hours, then served with Mashed 'Nips' and a glass or two of whisky.

Haggis pudding

Metric

For the suet pastry:
225 g self-raising flour
1 × 5 ml spoon salt
100 g shredded beef suet
Scant 150 ml water

For the filling:
2 × 15 ml spoons cooking oil
2 medium-sized onions,
peeled and finely chopped
225 g lamb's liver, sliced
225 g boned shoulder of
mutton or lamb, minced
50 g can anchovies, soaked
in milk for 30 minutes
100 g medium oatmeal
100 g shredded beef suet
2 × 15 ml spoons finely
chopped parsley
Finely grated rind and
juice of 1 lemon
Salt and freshly ground
black pepper
About 4 × 15 ml spoons
red wine or beef stock

Imperial

For the suet pastry:
8 oz self-raising flour
1 teaspoon salt
4 oz shredded beef suet
Scant ¼ pint water

For the filling:
2 tablespoons cooking oil
2 medium-sized onions,
peeled and finely chopped
8 oz lamb's liver, sliced
8 oz boned shoulder of
mutton or lamb, minced
2 oz can anchovies, soaked
in milk for 30 minutes
4 oz medium oatmeal
4 oz shredded beef suet
2 tablespoons finely
chopped parsley
Finely grated rind and
juice of 1 lemon
Salt and freshly ground
black pepper
About 4 tablespoons red
wine or beef stock

Cooking Time: $2\frac{3}{4}$ hours

To make a traditional haggis it is necessary to have a sheep's pluck (lights, liver and heart) and stomach bag, both of which are difficult to obtain. This is an adaption of the traditional haggis, and is steamed in a pudding basin. It should be served with plenty of rich brown gravy, mashed 'nips' and jacket baked potatoes.

To make the pastry: sieve the flour and salt into a mixing bowl. Stir in the shredded suet. Mix in the water gradually to form a smooth elastic dough that leaves the sides of the bowl. Turn out on to a floured board, knead lightly, then roll into a circle large enough to line the inside of a 1 l (2 pint) pudding basin. Cut out one quarter of the circle for the lid and reserve. Grease the inside of the basin and fit in the pastry lining, joining the edges in the basin with water. Set aside.

To make the filling: heat the oil in a pan, add the onions and fry gently until soft and lightly coloured. Transfer to a mixing bowl and add the liver to the pan, with more oil if necessary. Fry the liver briskly until browned on all sides, then remove from the pan and set aside to cool. Add the lamb to the pan and fry until browned, stirring constantly. Put in the mixing bowl with the onion.

Drain the anchovies and mince with the liver until fine, then mix into the lamb and onion mixture with the oatmeal and beef suet. Stir in the parsley, lemon rind and juice, and plenty of salt and pepper. Add the red wine or stock gradually until the mixture is soft but not wet.

Spoon the haggis into the pastry-lined pudding basin. Roll out the reserved pastry for the lid and place on top of the haggis. Tuck in the edges and seal with a little water. Cover with a circle of foil with a pleat in the centre. Tie securely with string. Place in the top of a steamer or double boiler, or in a large pan of gently bubbling water, and steam for $2\frac{1}{2}$ hours. Remove from the pan, leave to rest 5 minutes, then remove coverings and turn haggis out on to a warmed serving platter; or serve straight from the pudding basin. Serve immediately. Serves 6–8

Haggis pudding; Mashed 'nips

Mashed 'nips'

Metric

About 1½–1¾ kg turnips or swedes, peeled and diced
Salt
50 g butter
4 × 15 ml spoons single cream or top of the milk
1 × 5 ml spoon ground ginger
Freshly ground black pepper

Imperial

About 3–3½ lb turnips or swedes, peeled and diced
Salt
2 oz butter
4 tablespoons single cream or top of the milk
1 teaspoon ground ginger
Freshly ground black pepper

Cooking Time: 30 minutes

In Scotland, turnips and swedes are very popular winter vegetables, as well as being the traditional accompaniment to haggis on Burns' Night.

Cook the turnips or swedes in boiling salted water for approximately 25 minutes or until quite tender. Drain, then mash thoroughly with a potato masher or purée in an electric blender. Stir or work in the butter, then pour in the cream or top of the milk with the ginger, and salt and pepper to taste. Return to the rinsed-out pan and reheat gently. Transfer to a hot serving dish and serve.
Serves 6

85

Shrove Tuesday precedes the first day of Lent–between February 2nd and March 8th–and the story goes that pancakes were made on this day because housewives were anxious to use up all the eggs and butter in the house before Lent. Nowadays, few people abstain from eating these foods during Lent, but the custom of eating pancakes on Shrove Tuesday still survives, and pancake races are very popular.

Pancakes (Crêpes)

Metric	Imperial
100 g flour	4 oz flour
½ teaspoon spoon salt	½ teaspoon salt
1 egg, beaten	1 egg, beaten
300 ml milk	½ pint milk
2 × 15 ml spoons cooking oil	2 tablespoons cooking oil
To serve:	To serve:
Caster sugar for sprinkling	Caster sugar for sprinkling
3 lemons, quartered	3 lemons, quartered

Cooking Time: 15 minutes

The secret of making good pancakes lies in having a good quality, heavy-based pan for frying, and it is a good idea to keep one pan specially for cooking pancakes. The oil should be very hot, and a very small amount of batter should be used for each pancake so they are paper thin. Sieve the flour and salt into a mixing bowl. Make a well in the centre and put in the egg. Gradually add half the milk, beating in the flour vigorously until a thick batter is formed. Pour in the remaining milk and 1 × 5 ml (1 teaspoon) of the oil and beat until quite smooth.

Heat a little of the remaining oil in an 18 cm (7 in) pancake or frying pan and, when very hot, pour in approximately 2 × 15 ml spoons (2 tablespoons) batter. Tilt the pan quickly so that the batter runs over the bottom of the pan. Cook over high heat until the underneath is golden brown. Toss the pancake or turn over with a palette knife, and cook on the other side until golden brown. Slide the pancake out on to a hot plate, cover with another plate and keep warm in the oven while cooking the remaining pancakes in the same way.

To serve sprinkle each pancake with sugar to taste, roll up, arrange on a warmed serving platter and sprinkle with a little more sugar. Place the lemon quarters around the edge of the platter.

To freeze: interleave pancakes with freezer tissue or foil, then wrap stack of pancakes in foil or a freezer bag. Seal, label and freeze.

To thaw: unwrap and leave at room temperature for approximately 20 minutes, then reheat.

Makes 10–12

Pancakes; Savoury pancakes

Savoury pancakes

Metric

For the filling:
2 × 15 ml spoons cooking oil
1 large onion, peeled and
finely chopped
350 g minced beef
50 g can anchovies,
drained and soaked in
milk for 30 minutes
1 × 5 ml spoon dill powder
2 × 15 ml spoons tomato
purée
300 ml soured cream
About 8 × 15 ml spoons
beef stock to moisten
Freshly ground black
pepper
600 ml pancake batter
(see left)

Imperial

For the filling:
2 tablespoons cooking oil
1 large onion, peeled and
finely chopped
12 oz minced beef
2 oz can anchovies,
drained and soaked in
milk for 30 minutes
1 teaspoon dill powder
2 tablespoons tomato
purée
½ pint soured cream
About 8 tablespoons
beef stock to moisten
Freshly ground black
pepper
1 pint pancake batter
(see left)

Cooking Time: 30 to 40 minutes

Heat the oil in a pan, add the onion and cook gently for approximately 5 minutes until soft and lightly coloured. Add the minced beef and cook until browned, stirring occasionally.

Drain the anchovies and pound to a paste with a pestle and mortar. Add to the pan with the dill, tomato purée and 2 × 15 ml spoons (2 tablespoons) soured cream. Stir well to combine and add enough stock to moisten. Season with plenty of pepper, then cook very gently for 20 minutes, stirring occasionally. Taste and adjust seasoning. Meanwhile, make the pancakes, using twice as much batter for each pancake as stated in the recipe for pancakes (*above*). Keep each pancake warm while making the remainder. When all the pancakes are made, lay each one flat on a board, put a few spoonfuls of filling on each, then roll up and place on a warmed serving platter. Keep warm while filling and rolling the remainder.

Heat the remaining soured cream until bubbling, pour over the pancakes and serve immediately.

To freeze: pack in a single layer in a foil container without soured cream topping. Cover, seal, label and freeze.

To thaw: reheat pancakes from frozen in foil container in a moderate oven (180°C, 350°F, Gas Mark 4) for 35 minutes until heated through. Cover with soured cream before serving as above.

Serves 4

All Hallow's Eve, as Hallowe'en should be called, takes place on the last day of October, and is a time when old superstitions are revived and supernatural forces are believed to be about. The celebration of Hallowe'en dates back to the times of the Druids who held their fire festival on this day. These days, Hallowe'en is reserved for playing such games as ducking for apples and burning the nuts, for making lanterns out of pumpkins—and eating jacket baked potatoes around an open fire.

Guy Fawkes' Night follows Hallowe'en on November 5th and up and down the country bonfires are lit to celebrate the disastrous Gunpowder Plot of 1605. Parkin is traditionally eaten around the bonfire and hot spiced drinks are passed round to warm the revellers on a cold November night.

Cheesy sausage rolls

Metric

225 g flour
Pinch of salt
Pinch of cayenne pepper
100 g butter or margarine
50 g Cheddar cheese, finely grated
1 egg yolk, beaten
Pinch of dried mixed herbs
225 g pork sausagemeat
A little milk to glaze

Imperial

8 oz flour
Pinch of salt
Pinch of cayenne pepper
4 oz butter or margarine
2 oz Cheddar cheese, finely grated
1 egg yolk, beaten
Pinch of dried mixed herbs
8 oz pork sausagemeat
A little milk to glaze

Cooking Time: 25–30 minutes
Oven: 200°C, 400°F, Gas Mark 6;
180°C, 350°F, Gas Mark 4

Cheese-flavoured shortcrust pastry gives sausage rolls added interest. The pastry is very rich, therefore make individual rolls as small as possible.

Sieve the flour, salt and cayenne pepper into a bowl. Add the butter or margarine in pieces and rub together with the fingertips until the mixture resembles fine breadcrumbs. Stir in the grated cheese and egg yolk and draw the mixture together with the fingertips to form a smooth dough. Form into a ball, wrap in foil and chill in the refrigerator for at least 30 minutes. Divide the dough in two and roll each piece out on a lightly floured board to an oblong shape approximately 10 cm (4 in) wide.

Mix the dried herbs into the sausagemeat, divide in two and roll with floured hands into long sausage shapes. Place the sausagemeat on the dough and fold over to enclose. Brush the edges with a little milk and press firmly to seal. Brush all over the dough with milk, then cut into 2·5 to 5 cm (1 to 2 in) lengths.

Place the sausage rolls on a baking sheet and bake just above the centre of a fairly hot oven for 15 minutes. Reduce the heat to moderate and continue baking for another 10 to 15 minutes until the pastry is golden brown and crisp. Remove from the oven, transfer to a warmed serving platter and serve warm.

Makes about 15–20

Cheesy sausage rolls; Fruity parkin

Fruity parkin

Metric

75 g butter or margarine
100 g dark soft brown
sugar
150 g Golden Syrup
75 g black treacle
Finely grated rind and
juice of 1 lemon
175 g self-raising flour
Pinch of salt
2 × 5 ml spoons ground
ginger
175 g medium oatmeal
4 dried apricots, soaked
overnight drained and
finely chopped
50 g sultanas
50 g pitted dates, chopped
About 6 × 15 ml spoons
milk

Imperial

3 oz butter or margarine
4 oz dark soft brown
sugar
5 oz Golden Syrup
3 oz black treacle
Finely grated rind and
juice of 1 lemon
6 oz self-raising flour
Pinch of salt
2 teaspoons ground
ginger
6 oz medium oatmeal
4 dried apricots, soaked
overnight drained and
finely chopped
2 oz sultanas
2 oz pitted dates, chopped
About 6 tablespoons
milk

Cooking Time: 45 minutes
Oven: 180°C, 350°F, Gas Mark 4

Always store parkin in an airtight tin for at least three days before cutting and eating. The parkin will become more moist the longer it is kept.

Put the butter or margarine, sugar, syrup and treacle in a saucepan and heat gently until dissolved, stirring occasionally. Remove from the heat and stir in the lemon rind and juice.

Sieve the flour, salt and ginger into a bowl, then stir in the oatmeal and dried fruit. Stir in the melted mixture, then enough milk to make a soft dropping consistency. Beat well to combine. Grease a 22·5 × 14 × 5 cm (9 × 5½ × 2 in) baking tin and line the base with greased greaseproof paper. Pour in the parkin and bake in a moderate oven for approximately 45 minutes until firm to the touch. Remove from the oven, leave to cool in the tin for a few minutes, then turn out on to a wire rack. Leave until completely cold, then peel off the greaseproof paper and store in an airtight tin.

Cuts into about 12 pieces

Bonfire toffee

Metric	Imperial
100 g butter	*4 oz butter*
225 g soft brown sugar	*8 oz soft brown sugar*
225 g Golden Syrup	*8 oz Golden Syrup*
Walnut halves	*Walnut halves*

Cooking Time: 15–20 minutes

Use the largest saucepan available for making toffee as this will help prevent the toffee boiling over and sticking to the top of the cooker.

Brush a large shallow tin with a little of the butter and set aside.

Put the remaining butter in a saucepan and heat gently until melted. Add the sugar and syrup and heat gently until the sugar has dissolved, stirring occasionally. Increase the heat and boil the mixture rapidly for approximately 10 minutes until the temperature reaches 155°C (310°F) on a sugar thermometer. Remove from the heat and pour into the prepared tin. Leave to cool for 10 to 15 minutes, then mark into squares and put a walnut half in the middle of each. Leave until completely cold, then remove the squares of toffee from the tin and store in an airtight container.

Makes about $\frac{1}{2}$ kg (1 lb)

Bonfire toffee; Toffee apples

Toffee apples

Metric	Imperial
10 dessert apples, washed and dried	10 dessert apples, washed and dried
10 wooden sticks	10 wooden sticks

For the toffee:

Metric	Imperial
350 g soft brown sugar	12 oz soft brown sugar
50 g butter	2 oz butter
100 g Golden Syrup	4 oz Golden Syrup
1 × 5 ml spoon lemon juice	1 teaspoon lemon juice
150 ml water	¼ pint water

Cooking Time: about 20 minutes

Remove the stalks from the apples and push a wooden stick into each one.

Put all the ingredients for the toffee into a heavy-based saucepan and heat gently until dissolved, stirring occasionally. Increase the heat and boil rapidly, without stirring, until the toffee reaches a temperature of 145°C/290°F on a sugar thermometer. Remove from the heat. Carefully dip the apples in the toffee one at a time. Make sure that they are completely covered in the toffee, then plunge into a bowl of cold water. Stand on well-oiled greaseproof paper until set.

Makes 10

On the fourth Thursday in November the Americans and Canadians celebrate Thanksgiving Day. All over North America housewives prepare celebration dinners of roast turkey with all the trimmings: stuffing, cranberry sauce, roast or glazed sweet potatoes and buttered Brussels sprouts. The traditional dessert for Thanksgiving Day is Pumpkin Pie, an unusual combination of puréed pumpkin, sugar, eggs and spices in a pastry case. The menu given here is a traditional Thanksgiving one, but the recipe for roast turkey can obviously be used for Christmas Day.

Roast turkey with stuffings

Metric

*1 oven-ready turkey
(about 5–6 kg), with the
giblets
50 g butter, softened
Salt and freshly ground
black pepper*

For the sausagement and
herb stuffing:
*15 g butter
1 large onion, peeled
and finely chopped
225 g pork sausagemeat
100 g fresh white
breadcrumbs
2 × 5 ml spoons dried
mixed herbs
1 × 15 ml spoon finely
chopped parsley
1 egg, beaten
Salt and freshly ground
black pepper*

For the bacon and corn
stuffing:
*15 g butter
1 large onion, peeled
and finely chopped
225 g streaky bacon,
rinds removed and chopped
226 g packet frozen
sweetcorn
Salt
50 g shredded beef suet
100 g fresh white
breadcrumbs
1 egg, beaten
Freshly ground black
pepper*

Imperial

*1 oven-ready turkey
(about 10–12 lb), with the
giblets
2 oz butter, softened
Salt and freshly ground
black pepper*

For the sausagemeat and
herb stuffing:
*½ oz butter
1 large onion, peeled
and finely chopped
8 oz pork sausagemeat
4 oz fresh white
breadcrumbs
2 teaspoons dried mixed
herbs
1 tablespoon finely
chopped parsley
1 egg, beaten
Salt and freshly ground
black pepper*

For the bacon and corn
stuffing:
*½ oz butter
1 large onion, peeled
and finely chopped
8 oz streaky bacon,
rinds removed and chopped
8 oz packet frozen
sweetcorn
Salt
2 oz shredded beef suet
4 oz fresh white
breadcrumbs
1 egg, beaten
Freshly ground black
pepper*

Cooking Time: $3\frac{3}{4}$–4 hours
Oven: 170°C, 325°F, Gas Mark 3

If only one stuffing is liked, then double the quantity given here and use in both neck and body cavities. Any leftover mixture can be formed into small balls, rolled in flour and fried until crisp, then arranged around the bird on the serving platter.

Wash the turkey inside and out and dry thoroughly. Spoon the prepared stuffings into the bird – sausagemeat and herb in the body cavity, bacon and corn in the neck end. Sew both openings with trussing string and secure with skewers if necessary. Brush all over the turkey with softened butter and sprinkle liberally with salt and pepper. Cover with greased greaseproof paper or foil and place on a rack in a roasting pan. Roast in a warm oven for $3\frac{3}{4}$ to 4 hours, basting and turning occasionally. Remove the greaseproof or foil 15 minutes before the end of cooking time if a crisp brown skin is liked. To test if done: pierce the thickest part of the thigh with a skewer – the juices should run clear, not pink. Transfer the turkey to a warmed serving platter and remove strings, and skewers if used. Serve with gravy made from the giblets and cooking juices from the bird, jacket baked or roast potatoes, chipolata sausages and a selection of seasonal vegetables.

To make the sausagemeat and herb stuffing: melt butter in a pan, add the onion and cook gently until soft and lightly coloured. Transfer to a bowl, stir in the remaining stuffing ingredients with plenty of salt and pepper and mix thoroughly.

To make the bacon and corn stuffing: melt butter in a pan, add the onion and cook gently until soft and lightly coloured. Remove the onion from the pan with a slotted spoon and put in a bowl. Add the bacon to the pan, cook until crisp and golden, then transfer to the bowl. Cook the sweetcorn in boiling salted water for 5 minutes, then drain and add to the bowl with the remaining stuffing ingredients. Season to taste with salt and pepper and mix thoroughly.

Serves 10–12

Pumpkin pie

Metric

For the pastry:
225 g flour
Pinch of salt
65 g butter or margarine
50 g lard
2 × 15 ml spoons caster sugar
Finely grated rind of 1 lemon
1–2 × 15 ml spoons cold water

For the filling:
454 g can unseasoned pumpkin purée
1 small can evaporated milk (equivalent to 450 ml)
2 × 15 ml spoons honey
100 g soft brown sugar
Juice of 1 lemon
1 × 5 ml spoon ground ginger
1 × 5 ml spoon ground cinnamon
½ teaspoon grated nutmeg
Pinch of salt
2 eggs, beaten

Imperial

For the pastry:
8 oz flour
Pinch of salt
2 oz butter or margarine
2 oz lard
2 tablespoons caster sugar
Finely grated rind of 1 lemon
1–2 tablespoons cold water

For the filling:
16 oz can unseasoned pumpkin purée
1 small can evaporated milk (equivalent to ¾ pint)
2 tablespoons honey
4 oz soft brown sugar
Juice of 1 lemon
1 teaspoon ground ginger
1 teaspoon ground cinnamon
½ teaspoon grated nutmeg
Pinch of salt
2 eggs, beaten

Cooking Time: 45 minutes
Oven: 190°C, 375°F, Gas Mark 5

Although this pie can be made with fresh pumpkin, it is often difficult to obtain – and time-consuming to cook and purée. Cans of unseasoned pumpkin purée are stocked all year round at good grocers and delicatessens. Sieve the flour and salt into a bowl. Add the butter or margarine and lard in pieces and rub into the flour with the fingertips until the mixture resembles fine breadcrumbs. Stir in the sugar and lemon rind and enough cold water to bind the mixture together. Form into a ball, wrap in foil and chill in the refrigerator for at least 30 minutes.

Roll out the dough on a lightly floured board and use to line a 24 cm (9½ in) fluted flan tin with removable base. Reserve the leftover pieces of dough for the lattice. Place on a baking sheet, prick the base, then chill in the refrigerator for another 30 minutes. Meanwhile, make the filling: put all the filling ingredients in a bowl and stir well to combine. Pour into the flan case. Roll out the reserved pieces of dough and cut into strips to form a lattice on top of the filling. Seal with a little water. Bake in a fairly hot oven for 45 minutes or until the filling is set and the pastry golden. Remove from the oven and leave to cool. Before serving, remove from the flan tin, and place on a serving platter. Serve with plenty of whipped double cream.

To freeze: open freeze cooled pumpkin pie until solid, then wrap loosely in foil and overwrap in a freezer bag. Seal, label and return to freezer.

To thaw: unwrap and leave at room temperature for 3 hours.

Serves 6–8

Index